Essential Clinical Social Work Series

Series Editor
Carol Tosone
School of Social Work
New York University
New York, NY, USA

The Essential Clinical Social Work Series provides state-of-the-art theoretical and clinical knowledge for clinical social workers and other mental health practitioners.

Anna Morgan-Mullane

An Integrative Approach to Clinical Social Work Practice with Children of Incarcerated Parents

A Clinician's Guide

Springer

Anna Morgan-Mullane
Mental Health Services
Children of Promise
Brooklyn, NY, USA

ISSN 2520-162X ISSN 2520-1611 (electronic)
Essential Clinical Social Work Series
ISBN 978-3-031-28822-7 ISBN 978-3-031-28823-4 (eBook)
https://doi.org/10.1007/978-3-031-28823-4

This Springer imprint is published by the registered company Springer Nature Switzerland AG
The registered company address is: Gewerbestrasse 11, 6330 Cham, Switzerland

To my incredible parents, devoted family, friends, and the children and families impacted by incarceration who made this labor of love possible. You as a profound collective community have taught me how the power of one's own story can impact social change. You all used your own love and voice to champion for necessary revolution in the mental health profession, a profession I care so deeply about. This book is dedicated to all of you, may we continue to bring hope to many.

Preface

Despite the growing number of children and families affected by incarceration in the United States, there has been limited research conducted to explore the persistent psychological effects of parental incarceration on children. The literature finds that parental incarceration is associated with numerous systemic and racial stressors and trauma for children such as increased likelihood of experiencing harm from the criminal justice system (Huebner & Gustafson, 2007; Murray & Farrington, 2008; Roettger & Swisher, 2011), educational barriers, feeling isolated and misunderstood in academic settings, and grade failure (Murray & Farrington, 2008; Murray et al., 2012; Phillips et al., 2006). There are also reports of significant feelings of shame and stigmatization (Manning, 2011), and limited research addresses the social and emotional impact of having a parent incarcerated. In addition, there is little research aimed at developing best clinical practices—including educational and training requirements—for clinical social workers treating children and families affected by parental incarceration.

An Integrative Approach to Clinical Social Work Practice with Children of Incarcerated Parents is a guide for practitioners to recognize the phenomenon known as mass incarceration. This book provides an extensive overview of clinical practice models such as Trauma-Focused Cognitive Behavioral Therapy, Narrative Therapy, Relational and Behavioral Therapy, and effective anti-oppressive supervisory practices as the recommended solutions for treating trauma symptoms associated with children of incarcerated parents, their families, and their surrounding communities. *An Integrative Approach to Clinical Social Work Practice with Children of Incarcerated Parents* will enhance therapeutic relationships for social workers, teach innovative clinical practices most effective for this population, and offer a comprehensive discussion and understanding of the complex traumas faced both historically and presently by children and families impacted by the criminal justice system.

The numbers of individuals impacted by the carceral system are staggering as the United States is the world's leader in incarceration with 2.2 million people currently in the nation's prisons and jails, representing a 500% increase over the last 40 years (Vera Project, 2016). To underscore the extensive nature of this issue in US society, well over two million children have at least one incarcerated parent, according to the Bureau of Justice Statistics (Mumola, 2000), a number that is likely underreported because it does not consider the custodial states of individuals who are a child's guardian or who perform other significant caretaking functions (Manning, 2011; Miller et al., 2013; Murray & Farrington, 2008).

The number of children with parents in prison has increased 80% between 1991 and 2007 (Glaze & Maruschak, 2008). Nationally within state prisons, approximately 20% of children with an incarcerated parent are less than 4 years old, approximately 60% are between 5 and 14 years old, and 16% are between 15 and 17 years old (Turanovic, Rodriguez, & Pratt, 2012). One-third of all children will be 18 years old by the time their incarcerated parent is released from prison. For most caretakers, parental incarceration is a negative event; it can produce financial insecurity, elevate emotional stress, strain interpersonal relationships, and increase the difficulties associated with the supervision of children (Turanovic et al., 2012).

The need for a clinical guide on how to best respond to this primary trauma is due to the continual reports of emotional and psychological effects children carry who are directly impacted by the loss of a parent to the carceral system. Children exhibit the emotional effects of parental incarceration through complex trauma-related stress symptoms such as isolating themselves from their peers, anxiety, struggling to form healthy interpersonal relationships, concentration problems, sleep difficulties, emotional withdrawal from family members, substance misuse or dependence, and significant feelings of shame and secrecy. If unaddressed, the impacts of these symptoms can often lead to long-term psychological and emotional strain (Manning, 2011; Miller & Barnes, 2015; Murray et al., 2012; Phillips et al., 2006). Parental incarceration also threatens the future freedom of the children themselves by placing them at a far greater risk of experiencing systemic oppression that leads to pipelines to the prison and jail systems.

Children of incarcerated parents experience numerous sources of material and emotional insecurity and resource disenfranchisement. For example, children of incarcerated parents are more likely to be impacted by trauma from poverty, which impacts daily living and resources necessary to survive. Scarcity of food and rent is destabilizing, and families navigate harmful systems such as public assistance and experience residential insecurity through missed mortgage and rental payments (Cooper et al., 2009). These examples are symptoms of the greater socioeconomic disadvantage that exists for children even before a parent is incarcerated, and these conditions tend to worsen after incarceration (Miller & Barnes, 2015; Phillips et al., 2006). Besides these material consequences, a parent's incarceration can abruptly dismantle a family. Children of incarcerated parents are less likely to live in a home with both parents present (Geller et al., 2009) and are sometimes placed indefinitely in foster care while family members are sent to distant penitentiaries, making travel and visitation difficult for families with limited resources and few transportation options (Manning, 2011). It has further been demonstrated that our child welfare system is a key entry point on a journey though interlocking systems of oppression, a journey which more often than not intersects with another of our country's systems of racial oppression and surveillance which are part of the carceral system

(James, 2017). The drivers of this interconnectedness continue to be the colonial values that built the child welfare system, growing poverty rates and shrinking social service nets, hyper-incarceration of parents for petty drug crimes (e.g., war on drugs and the opioid epidemic), dramatic expansion in mandated reporting laws, and growing numbers of (traumatized) youth now aging out of foster care and being at increased risk of incarceration themselves. Clinicians utilizing this guide will more deeply understand their own role in harmful systems such as the "Foster Care to Prison Pipeline" (Juvenile Law Center, 2018) and referred to more broadly as the "Cradle to Prison Pipeline" (Edelman, 2009) or the *Family Regulation Pipeline* (Roberts, 2014) as they employ tools to actively dismantle the stigma and shame associated with losing a loved one to the prison system.

Parental incarceration itself can be seen as a symptom of existing trauma and/or a direct cause of trauma-symptom development. The overlapping racial, social, and structural disadvantages experienced by the majority of children of incarcerated parents will make it difficult to isolate the causal effect of parental incarceration on the development of trauma symptoms; even without this information, parental incarceration is a strong predictor of child trauma. Many children affected by parental incarceration experience complex traumas made manifest by sustained and repeated traumatic experiences like racism, poverty, diminished social mobility, lack of access to resources, and low employability that are increasingly common for poor, minority children (Wildeman & Western, 2010) and are found to be associated with trauma development (National Research Council, 2014). Even prior to their parent's incarceration, these children experience an elevated risk for trauma-symptom development and social marginalization (Wildeman & Western, 2010).

Formally, the most common clinical responses to addressing parental incarceration include the ecological approach, which aims to holistically understand the effects of incarceration on the interrelationships between the family members, environments, and society, and asserts that incarceration may produce multiplicative harms on children and families. These interconnected harms such as strained parent-child relationships, difficulties associated with traveling to and visiting custodial settings, community reactions to reentry, and stigma reinforce the negative sense of self-worth both by the parent and child. Because they experience intersectional sources of trauma, children of incarcerated parents are a highly traumatized population. However, due to stigmatization and secrecy, children of incarcerated parents are broadly viewed as an "invisible population" (Phillips & Gates, 2011).

Growing research on the number of children and adolescents impacted by the loss of a parent to incarceration requires that social workers and other mental health practitioners consider the unique clinical needs of this population and employ best therapeutic practices. Because Black and Brown communities are more likely to be affected by parental incarceration (Foster & Hagan, 2013), the specific clinical practices require practitioners to utilize anti-oppressive practices that maintain a full comprehension of past and present implications of mass incarceration—only in this way are we able to combat conscious and unconscious discriminatory behaviors and beliefs that exist within the social work profession and that perversely reinforce anti-Blackness.

In *An Integrative Approach to Clinical Social Work Practice with Children of Incarcerated Parents*, the clinical expertise and research of seasoned practitioners are conveyed through descriptions and implementation of clinical theory, best therapeutic practices, and qualitative research data to detail and explain the author's community-based practice model. Through the use of employable theoretical explanations and clinical illustrations extracted from the only behavioral health clinic in the nation specifically treating children of incarcerated parents, the author provides a revolutionary and integrative approach for clinicians, supervisors, and students to best treat trauma symptoms associated with parental loss.

Currently, there are no books about groundbreaking community-based models, efficacious therapeutic interventions, and clinical supervision practices to address the unique trauma stressors and symptoms experienced by children of incarcerated parents. *An Integrative Approach to Clinical Social Work Practice with Children of Incarcerated Parents* offers clinicians, supervisors, trainers, and students an overarching theoretical approach under which other analysis of practice can be explored and argued.

This book offers a unique, detailed look into the psychosocial implications and clinical treatment of trauma symptoms associated with parental incarceration. By describing the underlying theory, providing comprehensive explanations of available clinical interventions, and utilizing case examples, this book outlines best practices for clinical treatment and supervision modalities for clinicians working with individuals affected by parental incarceration. Furthermore, this book seeks to: 1) describe how criminal justice policy, specifically mass incarceration, impacts clinical social work practice; 2) demonstrate the collateral consequences and secondary impacts of mass incarceration on children and families; 3) provide a comprehensive description of the symptoms exhibited by children of incarcerated parents and how they meet the criteria for primary trauma; 4) illustrate an innovative community-based practice model which includes best therapeutic practices for children of incarcerated parents; and 5) provide practical guidelines to inform treatment, supervision, and training of clinicians and students. Designed to inspire and train social workers, *An Integrative Approach to Clinical Social Work Practice with Children of Incarcerated Parents* has a significantly wide-ranging application for both mental health and medical providers, as well as policymakers and practitioners. Individuals with clinical experience, such as social workers and mental health counselors, social work and mental health educators, supervisors in all social work settings, and clinicians interested in enhancing their work with children and families impacted by the criminal justice systems, will examine their practice and utilize the power of children and family narrative to improve and change their practice. The critical importance of criminal justice issues today suggests that a large secondary market exists among lay practitioners and policymakers within government and not-for-profit settings. This guide serves as a micro, mezzo, and macro practice guide for a wide range of professionals including psychiatrists, psychologists, mental health counselors, health educators, and social workers who hope to strengthen their understanding of the significant traumatic implications of mass incarceration on the children and families they serve in all settings

Chapter 1 offers a detailed presentation of relevant statistics and a description of the social and political processes that contribute to the development of mass incarceration; this first chapter lays the groundwork for the chapters that follow. The statistics presented quantitatively illustrate the effects of mass incarceration as well as the urgency of intervention for this growing population.

Chapter 2 explores how children exhibit the emotional effects of parental incarceration through complex trauma-related stress symptoms such as isolation, anxiety, poor attachment, inability to focus, sleep difficulties, substance dependence, and significant feelings of shame and secrecy. If unaddressed, the impacts of these symptoms often lead to long-term micro-psychological and emotional dysregulation and mistrust (Murray et al., 2012; Miller & Barnes, 2015). Many children affected by parental incarceration experience complex and systemic traumas such as racism, poverty, disenfranchised economic mobility, lack of access to resources, and barriers to employability (Wildeman & Western, 2010). This chapter also discusses the psychological, social, and emotional stressors faced by the guardians raising the children on their own and the strain of their own mental health and functioning on the child who has lost their parent to the injustice system.

Chapter 3 explores two specific theories researched within the Children of Promise, NYC (CPNYC) practice model, which include the *conspiracy of silence* and *ambiguous loss* as they relate to losing a parent to the criminal justice system. The conspiracy of silence is the failure to disclose to a child that a family member is incarcerated. This includes the hiding and shading of the truth that are commonly found in families affected by incarceration. This reinforces the shame associated with having a parent in prison and further complicates feelings of worry, anxiety, fear, anger, and dissociative responses to their parent who is now gone. This chapter provides a discussion on how clinicians can support lifting the conspiracy of silence through case illustration and step-by-step disclosure processes with clinicians and families, and strengthen the child's ability to cope and self-soothe when they feel dysregulated or angry about their parent. Ambiguous loss, which is commonly defined as a loss without closure obscures the grieving process for children of incarcerated parents. This chapter also validates the positive effects of this theory on clinical practice, and describes two common ambiguous loss types experienced by the children, both of which increase the internalization and externalizing of symptoms distinctly expressed and experienced by this population.

Chapter 4 provides an overview of Narrative Therapy when working with children of incarcerated parents. The chapter highlights how narrative practices shift the therapist's position as expert and make the child the expert in their own life as they begin to share their own lived experience regarding the loss of their parent(s) to the injustice system. The emphasis of this chapter is on understanding and making meaning that is revealed through narrative-based work and a child's ability to self-author their own traumatic losses. For children of incarcerated parents, who are commonly encouraged to hide or silence their painful experience of loss, narrative therapy is an essential and effective tool. Throughout this chapter, shared excerpts from participants engaged in this model will signify how children impacted by parental incarceration identify the changes they experience.

Chapter 5 includes an in-depth analysis of the development and utilization of Trauma-Focused Cognitive Behavioral Therapy (TF-CBT) with children of incarcerated parents. This chapter includes a justification for its utilization in community-based settings, focusing on the versatility and relatively brief treatment term, while describing the strengths and barriers of the modality for use with children of incarcerated parents.

In Chapter 6, clinicians are introduced to Prolonged Exposure Therapy as an impactful intervention to working with children impacted by parental incarceration as it addresses the necessary steps in a therapeutic reunification of family members when a parent returns home. This therapeutic model offers a phase-based guide to acknowledging and centering the trauma experienced by the parent who has been incarcerated and seeks to heal relationship processes that might be difficult for the parent when returning to their home and role as a parent while healing from carceral trauma.

Chapter 7 guides the clinician on how to use attachment and relational theory to undo problematic cognitive distortions and beliefs that are common to children of incarcerated parents. This chapter suggests this overarching theory as an intervention to support the child to use the therapeutic relationship and healing process within their own family to expand trust and gain a greater sense of safety in the world around them with those they identify as safe. The unique the traumatic instances are where a child loses a parent to incarceration requires the clinician to work in partnership with the child's attachment-based system when the threat of separation is experienced.

Chapter 8 illustrates the urgency for advocacy and mitigation practices when working with children of incarcerated parents. These macro practices for clinicians are encouraged when engaging with professionals within the injustice system such as judges, prosecutors, defense attorneys, and parole officers, and will educate readers in how to advocate for alternative sentencing and healing services. This chapter also draws on labeling theory to educate clinicians about how institutionalized social policies reduce the individual to their worst acts by utilizing dehumanizing and charged terms with negative connotations like "criminal," "murderer," "thief," "drug dealer," or "felon," while describing the importance of language to destigmatize these experiences and allow for individuals to be seen as humans and parents.

Chapter 9 emphasizes the use of critical consciousness (CC) and cultural humility as a continual and integrative approach to clinical assessment and therapeutic treatment planning in settings that service children of incarcerated parents. Critical consciousness invites the clinician to take a more engaged and relational role in understanding the institutional and societal effects on clients and to work to make changes in those realms through extensive reflexivity. Whereas clinical social work is traditionally thought to be a micro-level practice and the emphasis is on the therapeutic relationship, CC centers the critical interaction between the institutional effects of mass incarceration on the clinical dimension in therapeutic relationship and practice. Brief examples illustrate the parallel process that often exists in this situation for the child, family, and clinician to build a closer therapeutic rapport that builds trust and healing throughout the remainder of their partnership.

In Chapter 10, practitioners learn the most impactful practices to unpack their own racial biases and societal beliefs regarding those most impacted by the injustice system. This encouraging guide for clinical supervisors and trainers conveys the growth of awareness in both complex systems of oppression impacting the trauma experienced by the child that is unique to feelings and experiences associated with parental incarceration. The overview of Critical Race Theory (CRT) and Culture-Based Countertransference (CBC) emphasizes the clinician's ability to reflect, deconstruct, interrogate, and transform power in the therapeutic session by using racial trauma as its point of engagement.

Chapter 11 offers an assessment of the clinical theories, practice, and training centered in cultural humility and critical consciousness to underscore the most impactful micro and macro practices required to support and address the complex trauma experienced by children of incarcerated parents. This chapter concludes with the acknowledgment that all comprehensive practices highlighted throughout the book will amplify the narratives of impacted people, as well as empowering them and their experiences to inform communal healing practice and policy.

The conclusion, Chap. 12, stresses the call to action for practitioners working with children of incarcerated parents to embrace these micro and macro practices that aim to not only offer individual and familial healing but also disrupt systems of oppression that continually harm families due to policies and practices aligning with mass incarceration.

Brooklyn, NY, USA Anna Morgan-Mullane

References

Children of Promise, NYC: www.cpnyc.org

Foster, H., & Hagan, J. (2013). Maternal and paternal imprisonment in the stress process. *Social Science Research, 42*, 650–669.

Cooper, C. E., Geller, A., Garfinkel, & Mincy, R. B. (2009). Parental Incarceration and child well-being: Implications for urban families. *Social Science Quarterly, 90*(5), 1186–1202.

Glaze, L., & Maruschak, L. (2008). *Parents in Prison and their Minor Children*. Bureau of Justice Statistics.

James, K. (2016). A history of mass incarceration: Implications for social work. In *Forensic social work: Psychological and legal issues in diverse practice settings*.

Manning, R. (2011) Punishing the innocent: Children of incarcerated and detained parents. *Criminal Justice Ethics, 30*(3), 267–287.

Miller, A. L., Perryman, J., Markovitz, L., Franzen, S., Cochran, S., & Brown, S. (2013). Strengthening incarcerated families: Evaluating a pilot program for children of incarcerated parents and their caregivers. *Family Relations, 62*, 584–596.

Miller, H. V., & Barnes, J. C. (2015). The association between parental incarceration and health, education, and economic outcomes in young adulthood. *American Journal of Criminal Justice, 40*, 765–784.

Mumola, C. J. (2000). *Incarcerated parents and their children*. Department of Justice, Office of Justice Programs, Bureau of Justice Statistics.

Murray, J., Farrington, D. P., & Sekol, I. (2012). Children's antisocial behavior, mental health, drug use, and educational performance after parental incarceration: A systematic review and meta-analysis. *Psychological Bulletin, 138*(2), 175–210.

National Research Council. (2014).

Phillips, S. D., Erkanki, A., Keeler, G.P., Costello, E. J., & Angold, A. (2006). Disentangling the Risks: Parents Criminal Justice Involvement and Children's Exposure to Family Risks. *Criminology & Public Policy, 5*(4), 677–702.

Roettger, M. E., & Swisher, R. R. (2011). Associations of fathers' history of incarceration with sons' delinquency and arrest among black, white, and hispanic males in the United States. *Criminology, 49*(4), 1109–1147.

Turanovic, J. J., Rodriguez, N., & Pratt, T. C. (2012). The collateral consequences of incarceration revisited: A qualitative analysis of the effects on caregivers of children of incarcerated parents. *Criminology 50*(4), 913–959.

Wildeman, C., & Western, B. (2010). Incarceration in fragile families. *The Future of Children*, 157–177.

Acknowledgments

There are countless people to whom I owe a debt of gratitude for their guidance, passion, and support as I labored away on this book. However, firstly, I must thank all of the children and families at Children of Promise, NYC (CPNYC). Over the past 13 years, each individual and their authentic relationship and clinical partnership has deeply inspired my transformation as a person, activist, abolitionist, and therapist. Partnering with the children while holding space for their incredible brilliance to shine has been by far my greatest honor. Ms. Sharon Content, the Founder and President, has created an environment for children and families to strengthen their community through shared experiences that were otherwise silenced throughout the broader society. Lifting the conspiracy of silence for children of incarcerated parents has offered myself and incredible team members expansion in politicizing the therapeutic experience for individual combating the collateral consequences of mass incarceration.

This 13-year journey within a community of people who continue to mobilize in mental health settings would not be possible without the unbelievable team of Monique Newton, Paul Silverman, Annie Hirschman, Gen Uslander, Wade Caldwell, and Dr. Tyson Boudreaux. Their passion has motivated me to further my lifetime commitment to deconstruction work within the mental healthcare profession and commit to a life of creating courageous clinical spaces for individuals intersectionally and systematically harmed. Believing in a mission to amplify and center those most impacted by racial trauma within the carceral system would not be possible without the mentorship of Dr. Jae James. Dr. James is a visionary with his quest to dismantle systems of oppression that uphold and safeguard punishment practices in and out of prison and jail settings. His belief in the personal being political and the political is always personal has truly defined my commitment to ensure micro work centers macro change.

I would like to thank Carol Tosone, PhD, the editor of the Essential Clinical Social Work Series. She has served as an academic example to me over the course of my doctoral program, and without her encouragement and belief in the importance of clinical practice with this community, this critical conversation would not be available broadly to clinicians across the country. Dr. Stacey Barrenger served as the chair of my dissertation committee during my doctoral program at NYU Silver School of Social Work, where she supported me through countless hours of writing, research, and connecting more deeply to my lifelong fight against racial injustice, particularly communities harmed by mass incarceration. It was in my doctoral experience and relationships with Dr. James, Dr. Barrenger, Dr. Tosone, and Dr. Ruth White that I felt a burning passion for the clinical world to expand their knowledge and practice skills with a growing number of children and families across the United States who have lost their loved ones to the carceral system. I am forever grateful for this academic community convincing me to publish the writing and research stemming from my clinical and mitigation work which led me to the path of this book. My devotion to expand the clinical conversation to include racial trauma as a primary trauma in therapeutic settings has only been made possible by this team at NYU, the committed clinicians and staff at Children of Promise, NYC, and the activists and revolutionary organizers such as Arlene Adams and Five Mualimn-ak from Incarceration Nation. I would also like to extend my sincere gratitude to all of the children and parents who proudly contributed their stories and experiences as the primary tool for change in this book.

I would like to thank Janet Kim, MPH, of Springer for her incredible support throughout the process and the enthusiasm and patience as a motivator for the completion of this labor of love. I am beyond grateful that I have benefited from her time and effort. I have been so fortunate to work with the outstanding copyeditor who inspired this continual process and the momentum of work to continue with her humor, patience, time, and expertise, Susan Winson.

I would like to thank my colleague who generously offered to proofread chapters: Tiffany Owens. I would like to thank my healing community, Stephanie Niles and Mishie Owen. It has been an honor to be supported by you both throughout this entire process from start to finish, your words of inspiration were instrumental in this experience. I would also like to thank my wonderful friends Jeremy Cherson and Taylor Meyer for their encouragement, unwavering support, and joy throughout this journey. I am overwhelmed with gratitude to have so much love and encouragement in my life. Everyone listed above has provided me with the space to feel as though the mission and vision of this work is possible and that re-imagining healing can be achieved through hope.

About the Book

The veil of stigma and shame associated with having a parent in the carceral system perpetuates cultures of silence suppressing unique experiences of complex trauma. Children impacted by mass incarceration are identified as the silent victims of this epidemic, and addressing this primary trauma by centering this loss and the systems responsible for it will revolutionize our profession and practice. This book is a clinician's guide to understanding, unpacking, treating, and healing individual, familial, and communal wounds associated with parental incarceration. It provides guidance on healing complex trauma through phase-oriented, multimodal, and skill-focused treatment approaches, with emphasis on strengthening one's own narrative of power and pain while building community in supportive spaces.

By reading this book, you will become more familiar with integrative micro and macro healing techniques and modalities that are currently being utilized as anti-racist, anti-oppressive, and innovative practices. In addition, you will develop an understanding of and deeper unpacking of your own biases within the therapeutic relationship. New theoretical perspectives describe the integration of Critical Consciousness and Critical Race Theory, interweaving narrative therapy, Trauma-Focused Cognitive Behavioral Therapies, and contemporary integrative tools from Attachment and Relationship Therapies. The clinical assistance shared here can be applied in diverse clinical practice settings, with children, parents, loved ones, and community members.

About the Book

Contents

About the Author

Anna Morgan-Mullane, LCSW-R, was born and raised in Bellingham, Washington, USA, where she first found her love of community organizing rooted in her family values, with two parents who worked in spaces impacted by injustice. Dr. Morgan-Mullane obtained her Master's in Social Work from Fordham University and her Doctorate in Social Welfare from NYU Silver School of Social Work. After 18 years living and working within her community of Brooklyn, New York, she serves as the President of Mental Health Services at Children of Promise, NYC for 12 years and the President of Clinical Policies and Practices to Fresh Youth Initiatives in New York. Dr. Morgan-Mullane conducts an extensive training program for MSW and MHC interns, Licensed Clinical Social Workers, Licensed Mental Health Counselors, psychiatrists, and licensed creative art therapists that allows everyone to gain anti-racist and critical culturally responsive therapeutic skills needed to support individuals, families, and communities impacted by the injustice system, complex trauma, and intergenerational trauma. In 2012, Dr. Morgan-Mullane and Sharon Content successfully established the first outpatient mental health clinic in the United States specifically designed to address the experiences and narratives of children and adolescents impacted by hyper-incarceration. Dr. Morgan-Mullane has also developed clinical policies and practice guidelines and launched an evidence-informed treatment model which includes the employment of Trauma-Focused Cognitive Behavioral Therapy, Narrative Therapy, complex trauma systems theory, and Mitigation Practices. Dr. Morgan-Mullane's work explores the intersection of clinical social work, social policy, and systemic racism within all injustice systems. Dr. Morgan-Mullane is an adjunct professor in the NYU Silver School of Social Work and Simmons University, where she teaches several courses in Master's and Doctoral programs which she developed on the intersectionality of clinical policy and practice within injustice reform and abolition and mental health implications for those impacted by systemic oppression. Dr. Morgan-Mullane has presented her research over the last 15 years at the National

NASW conference in Washington D.C., NASW-NYC, Third and Fourth Annual CE Conferences, and at the Global Prison Conference in South Africa at the University of Johannesburg. Dr. Morgan-Mullane identifies proudly as an individual, therapeutic, and community abolitionist, as she believes the only way toward true healing will be through the reimagining of all mental healthcare systems globally.

Part I
Intersectionality of Social Work Practice and Mass Incarceration

Chapter 1
Why Criminal Justice Is Relevant to All Clinical Practitioners

Through a detailed presentation of relevant statistics and a description of the social and political processes that have contributed to the development of mass incarceration, this first chapter lays the groundwork for the chapters that follow. The statistics presented within this chapter quantitatively illustrate the effects of mass incarceration as well as the urgency of intervention for this growing population.

Nearly seven million adults are currently under some form of correctional supervision (Carson & Anderson, 2015), and more than two million young people are arrested yearly (Office of Delinquency and Juvenile Protection Services, 2017). Eleven million people cycle in and out of jail every year (Prison Policy Initiative, 2020). Approximately 70% of this incarcerated population has one or more children, and the percentage of incarcerated women who are mothers is even greater. This carceral state produces approximately three million children with parents who are incarcerated (Gelb & Velazquez, 2018).

In recent years, hyper-incarceration, also known as mass incarceration, has emerged as one of the defining civil rights urgencies of our time. The United States has less than five percent of the global population, but almost 25% of the world's prison population. That translates to a total of 1.46 million individuals in the country currently serving time (Friedman et al., 2016). The federal prison population has risen by more than 700% since 1980, and federal prison spending has increased by nearly 600%. That growth has disproportionately affected African American, Indigenous, and Latinx communities (Friedman et al., 2016).

Individuals involved in the injustice system also commonly come from and return to communities that experience higher proportions of what is known as "concentrated disadvantage" (Merolla et al., 2011). Concentrated disadvantage is described as more significant rates of homelessness, lack of access to effective and culturally responsive healthcare services, higher reports of substance misuse or dependence, and lower reports of educational attainment. These specific disadvantages extensively diminish access to opportunities such as education and

A. Morgan-Mullane, *An Integrative Approach to Clinical Social Work Practice with Children of Incarcerated Parents*, Essential Clinical Social Work Series, https://doi.org/10.1007/978-3-031-28823-4_1

employment. Many social workers and mental healthcare practitioners work in spaces directly addressing the disparities listed above. This chapter highlights the necessity of historical and contemporary legislation impacting the growth of mass incarceration as well as specific policy reform that has expanded clinical representation in re-entry and informed clinical program design and implementation for practice.

The knowledge of social policy, as well as the need to increase criminal injustice curricula and training for clinical practitioners, will strengthen the process of employing therapeutic models that destigmatize psychotherapeutic services and make treatment accessible, as all staff are trained in an anti-oppressive and culturally responsive approach to contextualize parental incarceration, mass incarceration, and their traumatic impact on BIPOC families. With this perspective, licensed clinicians will be able to utilize a broad range of clinical and environmental interventions to respond to the impacts of parental incarceration, advocate on behalf of families in court, work in collaboration with schools, and join parents in seeking academic, employment, and vocational opportunities, as well as support families in any other necessary case management needs related to their re-entry. Mitigation practices also serve as a primary therapeutic intervention to combat hyper-incarceration as a form of building a trusting and responsive therapeutic alliance. These unique clinical tools, which stem from the knowledge of and training in social policies that most affect families impacted by the carceral systems, demonstrate the need for more academic and training courses within social-work education across the country. The relationship to curriculum and direct practice will underscore the efficacy of research, for its use of evidence-based practices such as trauma-focused cognitive behavioral therapy (TF-CBT), narrative therapy, and relational therapy, as well as models that include attachment theory, conspiracy of silence, and ambiguous loss in working with children of incarcerated parents.

Historical and Present Federal Policy Implications for Clinical Practice and Education for Children of Incarcerated Parents

Social policies designed to address hyper-incarceration have significant traumatic implications for children directly affected by parental incarceration. Social work and mental healthcare practitioners have an opportunity to use their expertise in trauma-responsive care and brain development to further advocate for necessary reform to policy that adversely reinforces chronic traumatic experiences of over-policing and growing arrest rates in communities of color. The urgency surrounding mental healthcare providers to integrate an approach in which social policy and direct social work practice are combined improves the therapeutic alliance and anti-oppressive practice behavior in practitioners working with families impacted by hyper-incarceration. The requirement that direct-service practitioners (including supervisors) understand and analyze the effects of social policy on individuals will empower them to participate in the modification of harmful social policy.

These behaviors are operationalized at several policy levels: the personal, the organizational, the community, and the legislative (Branco, 2016). Practitioners must hold the belief that our social justice movements require consideration of all intersections of identity, privilege, and oppression that people face in order to be just and effective; as this is essential for full comprehension of the impact of these systems for clinical outcomes. Therefore, in our work with children of incarcerated parents, the training models and MSW curricula require training in how historical and present injustice and incarceration policies carry extreme weight in the feelings of fear and anxiety felt by children experiencing loss due to parental incarceration.

Absence of Criminal Injustice Courses in Graduate Education

It is estimated that only 10% of social work programs offer even a single course in criminal justice (James, 2016); therefore, it is imperative that coursework and training programs addressing mental healthcare implications and intergenerational trauma from generations of hyper-incarceration be required in the courses offered for clinical practitioners. Clinicians, supervisors, and clinical educators should be tasked with reinforcing the acknowledgement of this unique population with a renewed focus by social work educators on criminal justice and highlighting the need for a thorough evaluation of criminal justice content in social work education and trauma training. Less than 5% of MSW programs offer a concentration in a justice-related field, which typically consists of two to three specific courses and additional opportunities for field placement and/or research relevant to criminal justice (James, 2016). This suggests that many MSW social workers who ultimately practice in criminal injustice settings are not likely to have received specific criminal justice training as part of their MSW education, but rather learn how to negotiate the social work and criminal injustice interface through work experience within settings that may not be congruent with social work values and ethics. For those few graduate clinical students who have the opportunity to pair their field experience with in-depth training in how to operate within the criminal injustice system while maintaining a social work perspective, criminal injustice specialization has the potential to build a cadre of social workers as key leaders and innovators in the social work and criminal injustice interface.

Beginning in the 1970s, more conservative and punitive approaches to criminal justice policy, paired with growing skepticism toward the concept of rehabilitating "offenders," are cited as primary contributors to what has been characterized as social work's withdrawal from criminal justice. Although Reamer (2004) and others (Stoesen, 2006) assert that social work no longer has a powerful presence in criminal justice, others argue that recent trends, such as heightened focus on re-entry programming for individuals, the development of problem-solving courts, and an increase in alternative to incarceration programs, indicate a shift toward rehabilitation. The latter is creating a widening opportunity for social work that relatively few social workers embark on in their professional education with the aim of employment in the criminal injustice field. Virtually no courses in social work education programs focus explicitly or comprehensively on criminal justice (Knox & Roberts, 2016; McNeece & Roberts, 1997). Workshops offered at professional conferences or continuing education seminars rarely focus on criminal justice issues per se, and relatively little serious scholarship on criminal justice issues is authored by social workers.

Social work and mental healthcare practitioners offer significant potential for interaction between the two systems, which would advance the care required for children of incarcerated parents. Clinical researchers and educators who are experts in criminal justice predict a "re-emergence" of social work within criminal injustice, in both existing settings such as probation and correctional facilities and newly developed models such as drug and mental health courts and programs adopting a restorative justice framework (Gumz, 2004; Madden & Wayne, 2003; Roberts & Brownell, 1999; Treger & Allen, 2007). Trauma training for those involved in or impacted by incarceration and the juvenile justice system, as well as having field experience in criminal justice settings, is likely to influence post-graduate work in such settings for MSW students. With the shift in restorative justice systems, social work practitioners have rejoined the community in spaces such as re-entry programs, problem-solving courts, alternatives to incarceration programming, and trauma-informed care.

Since there are presently 11 million adults under some form of correctional supervision and over 2 million children are arrested yearly (Pew Center on the States, 2014; Sickmund & Puzzanchera, 2014), clinical practitioners have a strong likelihood of providing clinical care to adults or children who experience trauma associated with hyper-incarceration. This reinforces the urgency of providers to re-examine their education and training to be inclusive of how the injustice system disproportionately affects individuals who also experience several disparities that make them likely to seek support in social service spaces offered by social workers and mental healthcare providers. These disparities in relation to prior or current incarceration for children and families include poverty, homelessness, lower educational attainment (Carson & Anderson 2015; Wheelock & Uggen, 2006), substance misuse (James, 2016), mental illnesses (James & Glaze, 2006; Steadman et al., 2009), infectious diseases, and inadequate healthcare (Hammett, 2006). There are almost five times as many people in jails than hospitals who suffer from some form of mental illness while James and Glaze (2006) estimate that as many as 64% of incarcerated people have a mental illness. Many of these individuals also have comorbid substance abuse challenges—often utilized as a coping mechanism in lieu of treatment. Researchers also note that there exists a bidirectional relationship between homelessness and incarceration—each increasing the risk factor of the other (James, 2016).

The need for core curricula in clinical programs to include the collaborative discussion of social welfare policy in the United States and the clinical impact that it has on children of incarcerated parents is due to several policies that impact the 2.7

million such children in this country today. The most impactful policies for practitioners to better understand within their clinical application of interventions necessary for children of incarcerated parents include the Anti-Drug Abuse Act of 1986, Anti-Drug Abuse Act of 1988, Second Chance Act of 2007a, Fair Sentencing Act of 2010, and First Step Act of 2018. These policies and federal legislation impact both children and their incarcerated parents by virtue of the residual negative and positive implications of their outcomes.

Federal Legislation and Policy Reform Consequences for Children of Incarcerated Parents

Federal legislation that has caused significant racist and oppressive harm generationally to communities of color includes the Anti-Drug Abuse Acts of 1986 and 1988. This new legislation increased the number of law enforcement and presence of federal drug control agencies as well as drastically escalating mandatory sentencing. Rates of incarceration grew significantly from the Anti-Drug Abuse Act of 1986 (Pub. L. No. 99-570). Sentencing policies, particularly the mandatory minimum for low-level crack offenses, focus on low-level participants, giving them the same as or harsher sentences than for major drug offenses. As law enforcement focused its efforts on crack offenses, a notable shift took place in the incarceration trends for African Americans relative to the rest of the nation. This trend effectively transformed federal prisons into institutions increasingly dedicated to incarcerating African Americans (McCurdy & Vagins, 2006). As a direct result of this significant focus in sentencing, the Anti-Drug Abuse Act of 1988 (Pub. L. No. 100-690) specifically targeted crack cocaine as its major drug of focus. Crack cocaine was significantly less expensive than powder cocaine, thus making it more available to individuals with low socioeconomic status. The mandatory minimum sentences executed by the Anti-Drug Abuse Act of 1986 extend to generally viewing, as well as treating, all crack cocaine offenders as if their offenses were violent and involving dangerous behaviors or weapons, even though the research and statistics convey that most crack cocaine offenses had not been violent nor involved weapons (McCurdy & Vagins, 2006). Therefore, mandatory minimum sentences have resulted in significantly harsher and more harmful sentences for people of color, resulting in a disproportionate number of incarcerated parents of color in US jails and prisons.

The longstanding environmental and clinical implications that the Anti-Drug Abuse Act of 1986 and the Anti-Drug Abuse Act of 1988 have had on children of the incarcerated is profound. The first encounter of trauma for the child is when parents are first incarcerated. This results in the child becoming involved with the child welfare system or placement in some type of foster care, which becomes substantially disruptive to their psychosocial and physical functioning. Because 45% of African American children and 21% Latinx children have an incarcerated parent

(Sparks, 2015), this reinforces that children of color cycle through the child welfare system at much more substantial rates than their white counterparts. Wakefield and Wildeman (2013) reported that one-quarter of Black children born in 1990 had a parent in jail or prison by the time the child was 14 years old. Therefore, the increased rates of parental loss to incarceration due to the Anti-Drug Acts of 1986 and 1988 further suggest racialized trauma throughout policy practices in both the 1980s and 1990s, which contributed to the rise in hyper-incarceration and familial separation for children of incarcerated parents.

Transitions in legislation that became responsive to the growing number of individuals incarcerated throughout the United States include examples such as the Second Chance Act of 2007a. This act was passed by Congress with the intention of disrupting the cycle of jail and prison recidivism, through increased public safety and aiding states and local units of government, as well as Indigenous tribes, to better address the growing number of people who return to their communities without the resources necessary to succeed (Federal Prison Authority, 2014). The focus centers on four major areas: employment, housing, substance misuse intervention, and mental health treatment for individuals and families. The Second Chance Act of 2007a supported parents engaging in programming that offered mental health, physical health, and substance misuse interventions once they returned to their communities (H.R. 1593). This offered mental healthcare practitioners working with individuals who were impacted by incarceration ways to specifically prioritize the psychosocial distress and complex traumas within their community-based programming.

The Fair Sentencing Act of 2010 was signed into law on August 3, 2010, to reduce disparities in sentencing for individuals convicted of offenses for crack and powder cocaine (United States Sentencing Commission, 2015). African Americans were the largest population arrested and convicted for possession of crack cocaine; therefore, the Fair Sentencing Act directly impacted the reduction of racial disparities that resulted from the drug laws of 1986 and 1988 and their oppressive effect on people of color, specifically African Americans, communities of color, and children of incarcerated parents. Specific considerations within the Act highlighted the elimination of mandatory minimum sentences for simple possession. While the Fair Sentencing Act was structured to address the inequality in sentencing for crack and cocaine, it still employed racially biased language that overstated the relative harmfulness of crack cocaine:

> The familial reunification implications of The Fair Sentencing Act minorly aided in the racially disproportionate number of African American and other parents of color sentenced for crack and powder cocaine offenses (Harris, 2020). Consequently, reducing the length of time parents are separated from their children has a direct impact on the social, emotional, and psychological functioning of their children. This Act permitted parents the opportunity for their sentences for crack cocaine offenses to be reviewed by a federal judge and possibly reduced. (United States Sentencing Commission, 2015)

The First Step Act of 2018 was signed into law on December 21, 2018. The Act has three major components: (1) correctional reform via the establishment of a risk-and-needs assessment system at the Bureau of Prisons (BOP); (2) sentencing reform via changes to penalties for some federal offenses; and (3) the reauthorization of the

Second Chance Act of 2007b (P.L. 110-199). The Act also maintains a series of other criminal justice-related provisions. The First Step Act mandates that the Department of Justice (DOJ) must develop and employ a risk-and-needs assessment system to be used by the BOP to assess the recidivism risk of all individuals in federal prison and to assign programming to individuals in varying programming to address this "risk." Individuals who successfully complete recidivism reduction programming and engage in the assigned activities can be eligible for additional time credits that will allow them to be qualified for pre-release custody (i.e., home confinement or a Residential Reentry Center) earlier than they were previously allowed (James, 2019). The Act prohibits individuals who are convicted of any one of several offenses from qualifying for additional time credits but can permit other benefits, such as additional visitation time, for successfully completing recidivism reduction programming (James, 2019). The Act slightly modified mandatory minimum prison sentences for some convictions of drug trafficking with prior drug convictions by increasing the threshold for prior convictions that count toward triggering higher mandatory minimums for repeat convictions, reducing the 20-year mandatory minimum to a 15-year mandatory minimum, and reducing a life-in-prison mandatory minimum to a 25-year mandatory minimum. The Act made the provisions of the Fair Sentencing Act of 2010 (P.L. 111-220) retroactive so that currently incarcerated individuals received shorter sentences for possession of crack cocaine than they would have received if sentenced for possession of the same amount of powder cocaine (James, 2019).

The positive community and familial implications of the First Step Act of 2018 included parents having longer visits with their children during visitation hours, and many parents were allowed to return home once their sentence was reduced after completion of their recidivism programming. While there are several adverse oppressive barriers that remain in the oversight and implementation of assessing for what constitutes "risk" for an individual found within this Act, it has reduced the number of individuals in federal prisons since the enactment of the bill in 2018.

The Interface of Social Policy and Clinical Practice

The responsibility of clinical practitioners within the framework of policy practice aligns with the core principles and concepts of clinical practice, especially for those clinicians who are in direct service with individuals impacted by social policies addressing hyper-incarceration. The clinical lens and expertise of long-standing psychosocial distress of trauma associated with traumatic grief and loss provide valuable perspectives on the consequences of social policies that have contributed to the growing number of parents arrested and removed from their children's lives since the 1980s. People and their environments are interdependent and, therefore, aiding educational conversation to advocate shaping social policies in spaces where social workers can encourage change (e.g., schools, community, medical and mental health) will greatly impact the emotional outcomes of both children and their family members affected by the injustice system.

Traditional methods of developing social policies, much like social work or varying clinical interventions, are problem-focused and designed to detect deficiency. Similar to the medical model or direct clinical practice, social policy attempts to understand the problem as originating in the individual's pathology or working from the diagnosis and then prescribing a treatment. The role of the clinician is not that of a policy expert, but rather to ensure that policymakers take parents' and their children's perspectives into account, to act in partnership and to collaborate with individuals throughout the policy development process. Individuals must be included in the processes whereby lived experiences are shared, problems are defined, and policies are developed. Failure to focus on the individuals' perspectives can produce a continuum of devastatingly harmful policy. The strengths perspective is a stance that puts social work values into action.

A significant example of clinical and policy mitigation practices designed to disrupt adverse impacts of federal policy is highlighted within the case illustration below. Treatment planning was initially developed by applying the adverse childhood experiences (ACEs) assessment tools. ACEs are comprised of stressful or traumatic events, including abuse and neglect. They may also include household dysfunction, such as witnessing domestic violence or growing up with family members who have substance use disorders. ACEs are strongly related to the development and prevalence of a wide range of health problems throughout a person's life span, including those associated with substance misuse. ACEs include physical abuse, sexual abuse, emotional abuse, physical neglect, emotional neglect, intimate partner violence, substance misuse within the household, household mental illness, parental separation, and an incarcerated household member. Parental incarceration is now acknowledged as an adverse childhood experience, which is distinct from other adverse childhood experiences because of the complex trauma with shame and stigma that comes with having a parent in prison (Centers for Disease Control and Prevention, 2010).

Neurodevelopmental research has determined that a traumatized child's brain develops differently from the brain of a child who is emotionally healthy (Centers for Disease Control and Prevention, 2010). The emotional attachment between an infant and their primary caretaker influences both the structure and functioning of the developing infant's brain. Therefore, when a child experiences loss due to parental incarceration, the connection and reunification after disrupted attachment is central to a child's further development and healing process.

Case Illustration: Chris[1]

Chris is a 33-year-old father who was formerly incarcerated on a drug charge for possession of marijuana. He was given a sentence of 3 to 7 years as he had a prior drug conviction for possession of marijuana when he was 19 years old. Chris is the

[1] A pseudonym has been used to preserve confidentiality.

father of an 8-year-old son, 2-year-old daughter, and 13-year-old stepson. Chris and his wife were devastated by the sentence he was given and immediately connected to a community-based program to work with him on his case in an effort to reduce his sentence. Chris had already been at Rikers Island Correctional Facility while he awaited his hearing as he was unable to afford bail for 11 months and said he was "terrified to be sent upstate for seven years." During his year at Rikers Island, Chris endured significant physical abuse by other incarcerated individuals as well as psychologically abusive and racist treatment by the correctional staff. Chris's children were attending a community-based organization in Bedford-Stuyvesant, Brooklyn, specifically for children of incarcerated parents, Children of Promise, NYC. One of the services within the organization is to work with the incarcerated parent on any legal mitigation practices in which the clinician working with the parent's child would request to meet with the judge and legal team to discuss the traumatic experiences of the child as a direct result of losing their parent. Offering the psychoeducation regarding complex trauma experienced by both the child and the parent highlights the severe implications for behavioral and emotional stability. This necessary clinical information serves as a tool to promote shorter sentences for parents so they can return home to their children and break cycles of intergenerational trauma through reunification.

Through the agency, Chris's clinical team presented the mental health concerns for his youngest child, who had several suspensions while he was incarcerated and paralleled the relationship to his father as the primary adverse experience exacerbating his trauma responses both at home and at school. The clinical team also highlighted the cost of Chris returning home under the clinical supervision of the therapeutic program and how outpatient treatment with individual and family therapy would be more cost-effective for the state as the rate of incarceration was three times the amount of an outpatient program covered by his insurance. The social work team reported that he would still be serving supervisory time with the agency as it fits the "crime" that he needed to be "accounted for to the community," as reported by the District Attorney.

The judge ruled in favor of Chris spending the duration of his 3- to 7-year sentence back home under the clinical supervisory practices and reporting efforts of the mental health team at the community-based program. Chris would be provided with proper care in addressing his own cycle of traumatic responses to fear, anger, and low self-esteem that his son was now suffering from.

The mental health team convinced the DA and judge that they would be a part of the solution to decreasing the statistic of how many children become involved in the criminal justice system: they, themselves, would not have the proper opportunities to heal and have strong examples from their parents being home to address and heal from the trauma of the extended loss that was already in place. By providing weekly and monthly reports on outcomes of therapeutic sessions, treatment goals and objectives, school behavioral reports, and employment reports, the team was able to prove consistently to the judge, caseworkers, and attorneys that the alternative to an incarceration program was, in fact, effective and should be used in other instances where the goal was to decrease the likelihood of someone returning to prison. The team also conveyed that the statistics of these children not becoming involved in a similar cycle without the supportive efforts of mental health and wellness interventions through trauma-informed care would also not be possible without the presence and support of the incarcerated parents.

With the necessary education and training regarding policy impact and therapeutic intervention, the clinical study was able to present the problem formulation to the DA's office, which stated that the cycle of post-traumatic stress would continue through the separation of the father from his children, who were already presenting with symptoms of PTSD and causing disruption in school, at home, and with peers. By listing the alternatives to incarceration outlined within the First Step Act of 2018, such as supervisory mental health supportive services, substance misuse programming, and tailored services for educational attainment and employment opportunities, all under the supervision of the agency, the judge and DA accepted and approved Chris's return home with his family. The clinical neurobiological information on Chris's children's trauma responses directly associated with their loss in relationship to him proved as significant evidence to address the disruption necessary in breaking cycles of intergenerational incarceration by healing the individual through healing the family.

Reflection Questions

1. Can you define the following term: hyper-incarceration?
2. What do you think such a small percentage of social work programs focus on criminal injustice?
3. Why is it important for clinicians working with children of incarcerated parents to have a foundational understanding of social policy?
4. Do you presently work with anyone who is impacted by familial incarceration?
5. What are the implications of the Anti-Drug laws in the number of incarcerated individuals today?

References

Anti-Drug Abuse Act of 1986 (Pub. L. No. 99-570)

Anti-Drug Abuse Act of 1988 (Pub. L. No. 100-690)

Branco, S. F. (2016). *Revitalizing a counseling training clinic: Meeting community and student needs, Association for Counselor Education and Supervision (ACES) conference*, October 8, New Orleans, LA.

Bureau of Justice Statistics, Carson, E. A., & Anderson, E. (2015). *Prisoners in 2014*. US Department of Justice, Office of Justice Programs, Bureau of Justice Statistics, NCJ, 247282.

Centers for Disease Control and Prevention (2010). *Preventing adverse childhood experiences*. Accessible at: https://www.cdc.gov/violenceprevention/aces/fastfact.html?CDC_AA_refVal=https%3A%2F%2Fwww.cdc.gov%2Fviolenceprevention%2Facestudy%2Ffastfact.html

Fair Sentencing Act of 2010 (P.L. 111-220)

Federal Prison Authority, 2014.

Friedman, M., Grawert, A., & Cullen, J. (2016). *Crime in 2016: Updated analysis*. Brennan Center for Justice.

Gelb, A., & Velazquez, T. (2018). *The changing state of recidivism: Fewer people going back to prison*. The Pew Charitable Trusts.

Gumz, E. J. (2004). American social work, corrections and restorative justice: An appraisal. *International Journal of Offender Therapy and Comparative Criminology*, 48(4), 449–460.

Hammett, T. M. (2006). HIV/AIDS and other infectious diseases among correctional inmates: transmission, burden, and an appropriate response. *American Journal of Public Health*, 96(6), 974–978.

Harris, M. (2020). *Silent victims: Children of incarcerated parents*. Columbia University Press.

James, K. (2016). A history of mass incarceration: Implications for social work. In *Forensic social work: Psychological and legal issues in diverse practice settings*.

James, N. (2019). *The FIRST STEP act of 2018: An overview*. Congressional Research Service.

James, D. J., & Glaze, L. E. (2006). *Mental health problems of prison and jail inmates*. Bureau of Justice Special Report.

Knox, K. S., & Roberts, A. R. (2016). The crisis intervention model. In N. Coady & P. Lehmann (Eds.), *Theoretical perspectives for direct social work practice: A generalist-eclectic approach* (pp. 249–272). Springer Publishing Company. https://doi.org/10.1891/9780826119483.0011

Madden, R. G., & Wayne, R. H. (2003). Social work and the law: A therapeutic jurisprudence perspective. *Social Work*, 48(3), 338-347.

McCurdy, J., & Vagins, D. J. (2006). *Cracks in the system: Twenty years of the unjust federal crack cocaine law*. American Civil Liberties Union.

McNeece, C. A., & Roberts, A. R. (1997). *Policy and practice in the justice system*. Wadsworth Publishing Company.

Merolla, D. M., Hunt, M. O., & Serpe, R. T. (2011). Concentrated disadvantage and beliefs about the causes of poverty: A multi-level analysis. *Sociological Perspectives*, 54(2), 205–227.

Office of Delinquency and Juvenile Protection Services, 2017.

Pew Center on the States, 2014.

Reamer, F. G. (2004). Social work and criminal justice: The uneasy alliance. *Journal of Religion & Spirituality in Social Work: Social Thought*, 23(1–2), 213–231.

Roberts, A. R., & Brownell, P. (1999). A century of forensic social work: Bridging the past to the present. *Social Work*, 44(4), 359–369.

Second Chance Act of 2007a H.R. 1593.

Second Chance Act of 2007b (P.L. 110-199)

Sickmund, M., & Puzzanchera, C. (2014). *Juvenile offenders and victims: 2014 national report.*

Sparks, J. R. (2015). A social cognitive explanation of situational and individual effects on moral sensitivity. *Journal of Applied Social Psychology, 45*, 45–54.

Steadman, H. J., Osher, F. C., Robbins, P. C., Case, B., & Samuels, S. (2009). Prevalence of serious mental illness among jail inmates. *Psychiatric services*, 60(6), 761–765.

Stoesen, L. (2006). *Prisoner Reentry: Reclaiming the Challenge: Professionals Often Have Criminal Justice Backgrounds*. NASW News, P. 4

Treger, H., & Allen, G. F. (2007). *Social work in the justice system: An overview* (from social work in juvenile and criminal justice settings, pp. 44–52, 2007, Albert R. Roberts and David W. Springer, eds.--See NCJ-217866).

United States Sentencing Commission. (2015). *Report to the congress: Impact of the fair sentencing act of 2010.*

Wakefield, S., & Wildeman, C. (2013). *Children of the prison boom: Mass incarceration and the future of American inequality*. Oxford University Press.

Wheelock, D., & Uggen, C. (2006). *Race, poverty and punishment: The impact of criminal sanctions on racial, ethnic, and socioeconomic inequality*. National Poverty Center.

Chapter 2
Impact of Secondary Incarceration: Collateral Consequences for Children and Families

This chapter explores how children demonstrate the social, emotional, cognitive, and interpersonal effects of parental incarceration through complex trauma-related stress symptoms, such as withdrawn processing, anxiety, difficulty attaching to adult figures, disruption to focus, sleep barriers, substance misuse, and overwhelming feelings of shame and secrecy. If unaddressed, the impacts of these symptoms often lead to long-term psychological and emotional malfunctioning (Miller & Barnes, 2015; Murray et al., 2012). This chapter also discusses the psychological, social, and emotional stressors faced by the single parent raising the children on their own and the implications of their own mental health and functioning on the child who has lost their parent to the criminal justice system.

Identifying Parental Incarceration as a Primary Trauma

The United States is the world's leader in incarceration with 2.2 million people currently in the nation's prisons and jails, representing a 500% increase over the last 40 years (Glaze & Maruschak, 2008). To underscore the extensive nature of this issue in US society, well over two million children have at least one incarcerated parent, according to the Bureau of Justice Statistics (Mumola, 2000), a number that is likely underreported because it does not consider the custodial states of individuals who are a child's guardian or who perform other significant caretaking functions (Manning, 2011; Miller et al., 2013; Murray & Farrington, 2008).

Children can exhibit the emotional effects of parental incarceration through complex trauma-related stress symptoms such as isolating themselves from their peers, anxiety, struggling to form healthy interpersonal relationships, concentration problems, sleep difficulties, emotional withdrawal from family members, substance use or dependence, and significant feelings of secrecy and shame. If unaddressed, the

A. Morgan-Mullane, *An Integrative Approach to Clinical Social Work Practice with Children of Incarcerated Parents*, Essential Clinical Social Work Series,
https://doi.org/10.1007/978-3-031-28823-4_2

impacts of these symptoms can often lead to long-term psychological and emotional malfunctioning (Manning, 2011; Miller & Barnes, 2015; Murray et al., 2012; Phillips et al., 2006). According to the US Department of Justice (Mumola, 2000), without intervention, 70% of these children will experience the same racially oppressive systems of violence as their parent(s) and enter the juvenile and/or adult criminal justice system. Parental incarceration also threatens the future freedom of the children themselves by placing them at a far greater risk of future injustice involvement as communities remain over-policed and brutalized by violence from surveillance and mass incarceration.

Arditti's (2005) ecological approach to incarceration aims to comprehensively understand the effects of incarceration on the interrelationships between the family members, environments, and society and asserts that incarceration may produce multiplicative harms on children and families. These interconnected harms—strained parent-child relationships, difficulties associated with traveling to and visiting custodial settings, community reactions to re-entry, and stigma—have the potential to reinforce and be linked with one another. Because they experience intersectional sources of trauma, children of incarcerated parents are a highly vulnerable population. However, due to stigmatization and secrecy, children of incarcerated parents are broadly viewed as an "invisible population" (Phillips & Gates, 2011).

Parental incarceration itself can be seen as a symptom of existing trauma and/or a direct cause of trauma-symptom development. The overlapping racial, social, and structural disadvantages experienced by the majority of children of incarcerated parents will make it difficult to isolate the causal effects of parental incarceration on the development of trauma symptoms. Even without this information, parental incarceration is considered a strong predictor of child trauma. Many children affected by parental incarceration experience complex traumas made manifest by sustained and repeated traumatic experiences such as racism, poverty, diminished social mobility, lack of access to resources, and low employability, which are increasingly common for poor minority children (Wildeman & Western, 2010) and are found to be associated with trauma development (National Research Council, 2014). Even prior to their parents' incarceration, children of incarcerated parents experience an elevated risk for trauma-symptom development and social marginalization (Wildeman & Western, 2010).

The number of children with parents in prison has increased 80% between 1991 and 2007 (Glaze & Maruschak, 2008). Nationally, within state prisons, approximately 20% of children with an incarcerated parent are less than 4 years old, approximately 60% are between 5 and 14 years old, and 16% are between 15 and 17 years old. One-third of these children will be at least 18 years old by the time their incarcerated parent is released from prison. For most caretakers, parental incarceration is a negative event; it can produce financial insecurity, elevate emotional stress, strain interpersonal relationships, and increase difficulties associated with the supervision of children (Turanovic et al., 2012).

Children of incarcerated parents experience numerous sources of material and emotional insecurity. For example, children of incarcerated parents are more likely to receive public assistance, to experience interrupted phone or utility service due to non-payment, and to experience residential insecurity through missed mortgage and rental payments (Geller et al., 2009). These examples are symptoms of the greater socioeconomic disadvantage that exists for these children, even before a parent is incarcerated, and these conditions tend to worsen after incarceration (Miller & Barnes, 2015; Phillips et al., 2006). Besides these material consequences, a parent's incarceration can abruptly dismantle a family. Children of incarcerated parents are less likely to have lived in a home with both parents present (Geller et al., 2009) and are sometimes placed indefinitely in foster care while family members are sent to distant penitentiaries, making travel and visitation difficult for families with limited resources and few transportation options (Manning, 2011).

Parental incarceration also threatens the future liberty of the children by placing them at a far greater risk of future criminal justice involvement. Using data from Add Health, a national panel dataset that includes 20,700 respondents in grades 7–12, Waller & Swisher (2006) determined that paternal incarceration is highly and significantly correlated with increased likelihood of arrest before the age of 25. Huebner and Gustafson (2007) found that parental incarceration nearly triples a child's risk of future criminal justice involvement and that children of incarcerated parents are up to three times more likely to be incarcerated than counterparts who did not experience parental incarceration. A meta-analysis conducted by Murray and Farrington (2008) confirmed these findings and further concluded that these effects were exacerbated when the child was without additional protective factors, such as supportive communities, therapeutic outlets, or friends and family they can talk to, or if they reside within especially punitive school environments. There are significant racial disparities as well: in a sample of children who experienced paternal incarceration, Black and Latinx children were, respectively, 39.2% and 46.7% more likely than White children to be arrested before they were 25 years old (Roettger & Swisher, 2011).

The likelihood of future risk of involvement in the injustice system may be increased by other factors such as emotional distress stemming from racially oppressive systems through academic environments and lack of access to adequate health and mental healthcare, as well as lack of parental employment for the caregiver of the child. Parental incarceration poses an emotional risk to children, and, as early as age 3, children of incarcerated parents can begin to exhibit signs of emotional distress, such as aggression and difficulty attaching to primary caregivers (Geller et al., 2009). Well into adolescence and young adulthood, the emotional effects of parental incarceration can be exhibited in the forms of depression, anxiety, difficulty forming relationships, concentration problems, sleep difficulties, emotional withdrawal, substance use or dependence, and significant feelings of shame and stigmatization, which are all trauma-related stress symptoms (Manning, 2011; Miller & Barnes, 2015; Murray et al., 2012; Phillips et al., 2006). These emotional and behavioral symptoms have far-reaching consequences and may partially explain the educational under-attainment and school-based difficulties like truancy, being pushed out of school, and grade failure that are more common among children of incarcerated parents (Murray & Farrington, 2008; Murray et al., 2012; Phillips et al., 2006).

Growing research on the number of children and adolescents impacted by the loss of a parent to incarceration requires that social workers and other mental health practitioners consider the unique clinical needs of this population and employ best therapeutic practices. Because Black and Latinx youth are more likely to be affected by parental incarceration (Foster & Hagan, 2013), the specific clinical practices require practitioners to employ recognition of secondary incarceration within their practices, to help maintain a full comprehension of past and present implications of mass incarceration. Only in this way are clinicians able to combat conscious and unconscious discriminatory practices when exploring the traumatic impact of parental incarceration for children and adolescents.

Secondary Incarceration

Children and adolescents who experience grief and loss associated with parental incarceration have self-defined the critical social, emotional, and psychological experience of *secondary incarceration*, narratively defined as "having a parent be in prison on the inside while we have to live with the effects of prison on the outside." Gabrielle is an advocate and activist in Brooklyn, New York, who works in solidarity with abolition movements and agencies including CPNYC to help bring awareness to organizations and local politicians surrounding the secondary impact of parental incarceration on children. Gabrielle further shares in her work that "the prison we experience on the outside is the pain of not knowing how our parent is doing, when they will be coming home, if they're being treated okay, and there's nothing we can do to help them. It's our own prison."

In her work with children across New York City, Gabrielle[1] has compiled stories of personal pain that highlight her personal definition of secondary incarceration. Children express parallel feelings of uncertainty, pain, loss, and grief through examples such as, "They serve time on the inside, but we're serving that exact same time on the outside." These shared feelings of distress manifest through traumatic symptoms and expressions of pain, which remain strained with the physical loss of a parent.

Child development is substantially impacted by proximal relational experiences within immediate social contexts, namely, the educational and home environment (Bronfenbrenner & Ceci, 1994). Social, emotional, and cognitive development is influenced by ongoing social relationships within the youth's immediate context, as well as the systems and environments in which development occurs. Therefore, secondary incarceration substantially affects the value of healthy connections, as measured by self-report of perceived closeness and frequency of contact, between children of incarcerated parents and their imprisoned parents, specifically in regard to sense of self, personal safety, and emotional stability (Dallaire et al., 2010; Hagan

[1] Pseudonyms are used in this chapter to preserve confidentiality.

& Foster, 2012; Trice & Brewster, 2004). Children express traumatic stress in relation to their physical and emotional disconnection from their loved one due to prison, as well as the parallel trauma of what is known as *secondary prisonization*, when they are able to visit their parent in prison.

Gabrielle's work amplifies the voices of children who feel especially obstructed by oppressive systems both within and outside of prison walls. She conveys that the child remains in pain for as long as their parent is serving time. In one interview, Gabrielle explained:

> My father was up for parole but because the parole board decided that he was not eligible for early release, he had to finish his remaining seven years in prison even though he had done everything they asked, had letters from organizations, and was on good behavior for his last ten years. I remember a teacher telling me, "Well, at least it's only seven more years,' and I said to her, "At least? In seven years, I'll be in my 20's, and my father has been in prison since I was born. Seven years is not a 'short' amount of time for those of us who have been without our parents our entire life. Please don't tell me 'It's not that long' when you haven't been through seven years of not seeing your parent after not seeing them for ten years."

Children in similar situations to Gabrielle's have shared narratives of the discomfort of visiting parents in prison, expanding on the traumatic effects of secondary prisonization and how this compounded with secondary incarceration causes devastating feelings of isolation, depression, and rage. Gabrielle's narrative demonstrates the severe impact of loss on children when there is concrete awareness of where their parent is incarcerated and the length of time they are gone. There is significant awareness about the emotional, physical, and psychological impact of this loss self disclosed by the child.

Secondary Prisonization

In addition to the trauma resulting from the secondary incarceration, children experience further trauma as a result of their interaction with the corrections system. Megan Comfort (2019) identified this effect as *secondary prisonization*.

To define secondary prisonization, it is first necessary to expand on the process of prisonization for incarcerated individuals. According to Comfort (2019), incarcerated individuals take on the oppressive and violent culture of prison, including "acceptance of an inferior role," adapting routines, language, and customs of the prison, and development of "new habits of eating, dressing, working, and sleeping." Thus, prisonization can be broadly defined as the adaptation to the culture and role of being incarcerated.

Further, Comfort noted that this process is replicated for the incarcerated person's loved ones. Incarcerated individuals' "associates and kin are subjected to weakened versions of the elaborate regulations, concentrated surveillance, and corporeal confinement governing the lives of ensnared felons and thus are secondarily prisonized by their interactions with the penal institution." To navigate the rules and regulations enforced by the corrections system, families need to acclimate their behavior and presentation. Family and other loved ones' internalization of this oppressed role in response to the dominant police culture of the corrections system constitutes the process of secondary prisonization (Comfort, 2019).

In a case illustration of 6-year-old Kayla, her mother, Natalia, shared a recent incident at school where Kayla was "getting in trouble at lunch for refusing to eat her lunch with her class." Instead of inquiring about what was causing Kayla to refuse to eat her lunch, the administrators would "punish her and call to tell me she was not being 'obedient' and 'was defiant.'" When Natalia asked Kayla the day she received her third notification of the child's lunch refusal, Kayla explained to her mother that she had seen on the news that the adults incarcerated at Rikers Island were on a hunger strike. Knowing her father was presently incarcerated at Rikers Island, she took it upon herself to "join him in an effort to feel closer to him." When exploration of traumatic experiences is not properly assessed, children are often criminalized and racially pathologized as being defiant, disobeying rules, and being resistant instead of processing the appropriate responses in association with secondary incarceration and secondary prisonization as a necessary trauma response to the loss of their incarcerated parent.

The visitation experience also causes emotional distress in secondary prisonization. Starting with preparation for the visit to the experience in the waiting room to the actual visit with the incarcerated parent, this is the main focus of the process of secondary prisonization. Comfort (2019) described the taxing process of preparing to visit an incarcerated family member, from choosing clothing that will be deemed appropriate by the corrections officers to waking up very early in the morning to travel long distances to reach the prison.

Once Natalia and Kayla received the update that Kayla's father was going to serve the remainder of his life sentence just 10 hours from their Brooklyn home, Natalia reviewed all the necessary rules for clothing and gifts she would be allowed to bring. In August they took a bus overnight for their first visit with Kayla's father and when they arrived, they were told they "did not have the appropriate clothing" and "would need to change our shirts as they were apparently too short in the arm length." Natalia continued to explain that she read in detail what appropriate clothing would consist of, but the temperature was above 95 degrees that day and there was no air conditioning on the bus or in the waiting room. Because Natalia did not have enough money to purchase a new shirt as she had spent her only money for the trip on gifts for her husband, the administrators would not let her enter and told her she would "have to come another time." The devastation of not being able to see her husband and Kayla's father had a long-lasting impact on both Natalia and Kayla as they traveled the 10 hours back to Brooklyn. Natalia would have to wait another 3–6 months to save up enough time off from her place of employment to plan another trip. Natalia described how, after they were unable to see him for that initial visit, Kayla would cry for her father for the duration until they were able to see him again. Research has shown that contact visits for family members provide an opportunity for children to see that their parents are alive, safe, and well and to have physical interaction with their parents, which aids in the strengthening of parent-child attachment (Hairston, 2007; Tasca, 2016; Tasca et al., 2016).

Comfort described the family members undergoing the scrutiny of corrections officers upon arrival, sometimes having their clothing and presentation deemed "inappropriate," which "humiliates visitors, especially if they are chastised for being too sexually enticing." Furthermore, family members often need to wait long hours in the waiting room or even sometimes get turned away due to "erratic changes [to visitation policies] without notice" (Comfort, 2019). Once in the visiting room, family members must police their own behavior to ensure their visit is not terminated by corrections officers.

Ryan is a mother of a male-identified adolescent who worked extremely hard both financially and emotionally to maintain her son and ex-husband's physical relationship with visits to the prison where the father was incarcerated. Ryan describes her own experience with secondary prisonization as "neither fully captive nor fully free since I could walk in and walk out." Loved ones find themselves trying to balance self-modification and self-preservation in their efforts to pierce the carceral border, gaining short-term rights of entry while unwittingly preparing a foundation for the institution's long-term distortion of their personal, domestic, and social worlds (Comfort, 2019). Thus, the visitation experience, though it is the only chance for physical interaction between incarcerated individuals and their families, demands that the family members be subjugated to policing that enforces a process of secondary prisonization (Comfort, 2019). Ryan outlined in detail that the amount of stress she endured each visit was a leading factor in her decision to go without visits for some time in an effort to heal from her son's own traumatic responses throughout the visit. Ryan describes the following scenario as a regular routine visit within the prison system:

> We'd walk into the visiting room, which was usually freezing in the winter or too hot in the summer. It was like they wanted us all to be uncomfortable. I was already angry, tired, and irritable in the visit because being on that damn bus for 14 hours with a teenager is enough to make anyone crazy. When we came, [ex-husband] would often be late because there was usually a lockdown or a fight, so they had to keep everyone in their rooms for longer, and it didn't seem like a coincidence that it was during visiting hours they were usually mandated to stay in for a lockdown. When he finally came to see us, we usually would only have about an hour visit left of the three hours we were given. We were all so tired, there would be no activities for us to do since the waiting room had no resources for kids, no games, no books, only the vending machine. I could tell he felt bad that we'd travel all this way for one hour, we were tired, I was angry at how the guards spoke to me, and then before I knew it, the visit was over, and he'd be going back without being able to hug my son. It was awful, it drained us, and eventually we felt like we wanted to take a break from the whole process.

Ryan's narrative is one of countless parents who try to maintain the emotional stability of their children who struggle with the psychological inferences of both secondary incarceration and secondary prisonization. These forms of specific traumatic stress result in excessive worry, fear, anxiety, and ambiguity regarding the ability and inability of children to connect with their parents who are presently incarcerated. The strain caused within the child-parent relationship reinforces the essential feelings expressed by children of incarcerated parents that must be included in therapeutic and clinical assessment for expansive practice in treatment. The impact each secondary collateral response has on child development is critical for clinicians to consider when effectively forming best healing practices for children of incarcerated parents.

Parental Loss and Traumatic Stress Within Child Development

Neurodevelopmental research has determined that a traumatized child's brain develops at a different capacity than the brain of a child who is without emotional distress (Perry, 2006; Schore, 2000, 2002; Schore & Schore, 2008, 2010). Disruptions in typical development are associated with negative experiences, such as chronic (Felitti et al., 1998) or significant (Jackson et al., 2014) trauma and adversity, and with a range of challenging behavioral, emotional, social, and cognitive outcomes (Hambrick et al., 2019), and will have a lasting impact on the child's future development if they go unaddressed. Therefore, when assessing parental loss for an infant or latency-age child, it is critical to recognize the influence of this disruptive and traumatic loss and consider how both the psychosocial infrastructure and functioning of the developing infant's brain are at risk during development. Disrupted attachment impacts the brain structure and function, causing developmental/relational trauma. Developmental trauma is the result of abuse, abandonment, and neglect during the first 3 years of a child's life; this trauma is caused by a relational disconnect between a child and mother that is either too long or too frequent during ordinary normal or subtle daily activities (Perry, 2006; Schore, 2000, 2002, Schore & Schore, 2008, 2010). Prior work has demonstrated that healthy self-organization of the developing neural networks happens in the context of the child's relationship with the primary caregiver (Schore, 2000). Children develop representations of relationships that are less optimal when attachment figures are unavailable due to discontinuity in care or the occurrence of prolonged separation. (Toth et al., 2002).

Consistent with attachment theory (Kobak, 1999), the majority of children initially reacted to separation with sadness, crying, and calling for or looking for their mothers. Other common reactions include confusion, worry, anger, acting out, fear, developmental regression, sleep problems, and indifference. Although many of these responses are similar to reactions exhibited by older children following the loss of a parent to incarceration, such as loneliness, fear, anger, and aggression, young children's sleep patterns and maintenance of developmental milestones appeared highly vulnerable to disruption. Lack of mother-child contact during imprisonment may result in children viewing the mother as unavailable when needed, which may have implications for children's representations of attachment relationships.

The mother-child attachment relationship is disrupted when a mother is incarcerated in jail or prison and, as a result, becomes emotionally unavailable to her children. Children of incarcerated parents are at risk for a number of negative outcomes, including primary caregiver disruptions, exposure to non-birth parents, economic disadvantage, residential mobility, shame, and stigma (Dallaire, 2007; Phillips et al., 2002; Tasca et al., 2011).

The following changes might also be seen in children of incarcerated parents: birth to age 2, absence of parent-child bond; ages 2–6, separation anxiety, barriers to full life cycle stage of social development; ages 7–10, challenges to establishing positive self-concept; ages 11–14, feeling unheard and devalued, pushing back on consequences; ages 15–17, premature disruption of relationship with parents.

When there is a secure attachment relationship, there is healthy opportunity for growth in neurological development. The adverse childhood experiences (ACEs) are stressful or traumatic events, including child abuse and physical absence through traumatic or abrupt loss. Parental incarceration is now acknowledged as an ACE and is different from other adverse childhood experiences because of the distinct intersection of traumas, including feelings and experiences of shame and stigma, that accompanies having a parent in prison (Centers for Disease Control and Prevention, 2010).

Reflection Questions

1. Can you define the following term: secondary incarceration?
2. What are the core differences between complex trauma-related stress and developmental trauma?
3. Do you feel the carceral visitation process on children impacts their grief and loss of their parent?
4. What are the implications of a child's decision not to visit their parent while incarcerated? If you were their clinician, how would you help them process their experience of secondary incarceration/prisonization?

References

Arditti, J. A. (2005). Families and incarceration: An ecological approach. *Families in Society, 86*(2), 251–260.

Bronfenbrenner, U., & Ceci, S. J. (1994). Nature-nuture reconceptualized in developmental perspective: A bioecological model. *Psychological Review, 101*(4), 568–586.

Centers for Disease Control and Prevention (2010). *Preventing adverse childhood experiences*. Accessible at: https://www.cdc.gov/violenceprevention/aces/fastfact.html?CDC_AA_refVal=https%3A%2F%2Fwww.cdc.gov%2Fviolenceprevention%2Facestudy%2Ffastfact.html

Comfort, M. (2019). Developments and next steps in theorizing the secondary prisonization of families. In *The Palgrave handbook of prison and the family* (pp. 65–79). Palgrave Macmillan.

Dallaire, D. H. (2007). Children with incarcerated mothers: Developmental outcomes, special challenges, and recommendations. *Journal of Applied Developmental Psychology, 28*, 15–24.

Dallaire, D. H., Ciccone, A., & Wilson, L. C. (2010). Teachers' experiences with and expectations of children with incarcerated parents. *Journal of Applied Developmental Psychology, 31*(4), 281–290.

Felitti, V. J., Anda, R. F., Nordenberg, D., Williamson, D. F., Spitz, A. M., Edwards, V., & Marks, J. S. (1998). Relationship of childhood abuse and household dysfunction to many of the leading causes of death in adults: The Adverse Childhood Experiences (ACE) Study. *American Journal of Preventive Medicine*, *14*(4), 245–258.

Foster, H., Hagan, J., (2013). Maternal and paternal imprisonment in the stress process. *Social Science Research*, *42*, 650–669.

Geller, A., Garfinkel, I., Cooper, C. E., & Mincy, R. B. (2009). Parental incarceration and child well-being: Implications for urban families. *Social Science Quarterly, 90*(5), 1186–1202.

Glaze, L., & Maruschak, L. (2008). *Parents in prison and their minor children.* Bureau of Justice Statistics.

Hagan, J., & Foster, H. (2012). Intergenerational educational effects of mass imprisonment in America. *Sociology of Education*, *85*(3), 259–286.

Hairston, C. F. (2007). *Focus on children with incarcerated parents: An overview of the research literature.*

Hambrick, E. P., Brawner, T. W., Perry, B. D., Brandt, K., Hofmeister, C., & Collins, J. O. (2019). Beyond the ACE score: Examining relationships between timing of developmental adversity, relational health and developmental outcomes in children. *Archives of Psychiatric Nursing*, *33*(3), 238–247.

Huebner, B. M., & Gustafson, R. (2007). The effect of maternal incarceration on adult offspring in the criminal justice system. *Journal of Criminal Justice*, *35* (3), 283–296.

Jackson, Y., Gabrielli, J., Fleming, K., Tunno, A. M., & Makanui, P. K. (2014). Untangling the relative contribution of maltreatment severity and frequency to type of behavioral outcome in foster youth. Child abuse & neglect, *38*(7), 1147–1159.

Kobak, R. (1999). *The emotional dynamics of disruptions in attachment relationships: Implications for theory, research, and clinical intervention.*

Manning, R. (2011). Punishing the innocent: Children of incarcerated and detained parents. *Criminal Justice Ethics, 30*(3), 267–287.

Miller, H. V., & Barnes, J. C. (2015). The association between parental incarceration and health, education, and economic outcomes in young adulthood. *American Journal of Criminal Justice*, *40*, 765–784.

Miller, A. L., Perryman, J., Markovitz, L., Franzen, S., Cochran, S., & Brown, S. (2013). Strengthening incarcerated families: Evaluating a pilot program for children of incarcerated parents and their caregivers. *Family Relations, 62*, 584–596.

Mumola, C. J. (2000, August). *Incarcerated parents and their children*. U.S. Department of Justice, Office of Justice Programs, Bureau of Justice Statistics.

Murray, J., & Farrington, D. P. (2008). The effects of parental imprisonment on children. *Crime and Justice*, *37*(1), 133–206.

Murray, J., Farrington, D. P., & Sekol, I. (2012). Children's antisocial behavior, mental health, drug use, and educational performance after parental incarceration: A systematic review and meta-analysis. *Psychological Bulletin, 138*(2), 175–210.

National Research Council. (2014). *New directions in child abuse and neglect research.*

Perry, B. D. (2006). *Applying principles of neurodevelopment to clinical work with maltreated and traumatized children: The neurosequential model of therapeutics.*

Phillips, S. D., & Gates, T. (2011). A conceptual framework for understanding the stigmatization of children of incarcerated parents. *Journal of Child and Family Studies, 20*, 286–294.

Phillips, S. D., Erkanki, A., Keeler, G. P., Costello, E. J., & Angold, A. (2006). Disentangling the risks: Parents criminal justice involvement and children's exposure to family risks. *Criminology & Public Policy, 5*(4), 677–702.

Roettger, M. E., & Swisher, R. R. (2011). Associations of fathers' history of incarceration with sons' delinquency and arrest among black, white, and hispanic males in the United States. *Criminology, 49*(4), 1109–1147.

Schore, A. N. (2000). Attachment, the right brain, and empathic processes within the therapeutic alliance. *Psychologist Psychoanalyst, 20*(4), 8–11.

Schore, A. N. (2002). Advances in neuropsychoanalysis, attachment theory, and trauma research: Implications for self psychology. *Psychoanalytic Inquiry*, *22*(3), 433–484.

Schore, J. R., & Schore, A. N. (2008). Modern attachment theory: The central role of affect regulation in development and treatment. *Clinical Social Work Journal*, *36*(1), 9–20.

Schore, J. R., & Schore, A. N. (2010). Clinical social work and regulation theory: Implications of neurobiological models of attachment. In *Adult attachment in clinical social work* (pp. 57–75). Springer.

Tasca, M. (2016). The gatekeepers of contact: Child–caregiver dyads and parental prison visitation. *Criminal Justice and Behavior*, *43*(6), 739–758.

Tasca, M., Rodriguez, N., & Zatz, M. S. (2011). Family and residential instability in the context of paternal and maternal incarceration. *Criminal Justice and Behavior*, *38*(3), 231–247.

Tasca, M., Wright, K. A., Turanovic, J. J., White, C., & Rodriguez, N. (2016). Moving visitation research forward: The Arizona prison visitation project. *Criminology, Criminal Justice, Law & Society*, *17*, 55.

Toth, S. L., Maughan, A., Manly, J. T., Spagnola, M., & Cicchetti, D. (2002). The relative efficacy of two interventions in altering maltreated preschool children's representational models: Implications for attachment theory. *Development and Psychopathology*, *14*(4), 877–908.

Trice, A. D., & Brewster, J. (2004). The effects of maternal incarceration on adolescent children. *Journal of Police and Criminal Psychology*, *19*(1), 27–35.

Turanovic, J. J., Rodriguez, N., & Pratt, T. C. (2012). The collateral consequences of incarceration revisited: A qualitative analysis of the effects on caregivers of children of incarcerated parents. *Criminology 50*(4), 913 – 959.

Waller, M. R., & Swisher, R. (2006) Fathers' risk factors in fragile families: Implications for "healthy" relationships and father involvement. *Social Problems, 53*(3), 392–420.

Wildeman, C., & Western, B. (2010). Incarceration in fragile families. *The future of children*, 157–177.

Chapter 3
Psychosocial Stressors for Children of Incarcerated Parents: Conspiracy of Silence and Ambiguous Loss

This chapter extensively explores two specific theories researched within the Children of Promise, NYC (CPNYC) practice model, which include the *conspiracy of silence* and *ambiguous loss* as they relate to losing a parent to the criminal justice system. Through case illustration and step-by-step disclosure processes with clinicians and families, this chapter provides a comprehensive discussion on how lifting the conspiracy of silence strengthens the child's ability to cope and self-soothe when they feel dysregulated or angry about their parent.

Conspiracy of Silence: Amplifying Collective Healing for Children of Incarcerated Parents

Many caregivers of children who have incarcerated parents commonly choose to withhold information regarding parental incarceration entirely or partially in an effort to safeguard their children's behavioral and emotional responses to loss. Caregivers have shared that, in an effort to guide behavioral and emotional coping strategies, they will also instruct children not to talk about it, even if they are aware (Parke & Clarke-Stewart, 2001), as a way to protect them from the negative responses from the broader society. This deliberate misinformation, either toward children or to outside society, has been referred to as a *conspiracy of silence* (Dallaire et al., 2010; Kampfner, 1995) or *forced silence* (Johnston, 1995). The continual challenge to help families feel supported through this process reinforces the invisibility that children already experience as a population in the criminal justice and welfare systems (Krupat, 2007; Simmons, 2000). Caregivers may be concerned that the truth will cause children to fear for their parent's livelihood more than a deceptive explanation would (Lange, 2000). A child's ability to cope with the unknown information related to the loss of their parent could be hindered by uncertainty and

A. Morgan-Mullane, *An Integrative Approach to Clinical Social Work Practice with Children of Incarcerated Parents*, Essential Clinical Social Work Series,
https://doi.org/10.1007/978-3-031-28823-4_3

information gaps, resulting in a higher degree of anxiety and fear observed in children (Johnston, 1995). This increase in fear or anxiety is supported by ambiguous loss theory (Boss, 2007), which states that the most stressful kinds of loss are ambiguous, as persisting uncertainties block cognition, coping, and grieving processes, thus preventing attainment of closure (Chui, 2016). Child development theorists demonstrate the need for children to experience honest and reliable information in order to begin the dual process of coping with loss and adjusting to new life circumstances of losing a parent to the carceral system (Chui, 2016). Therefore, given the current body of evidence, experts now recommend telling the truth as the best course of action (Arditti, 2012), which also guarantees that fundamental communication channels between the incarcerated individual and family members can remain open (Hairston, 2003).

Anthropologist Allan Young's research provides an extensive discussion on the relationship that trauma, memory, and psychiatry have in the conspiracy of silence theory. Young's work highlighted how the clinical practices within an inpatient treatment program for Vietnam veterans with post-traumatic stress disorder (PTSD) were designed within the grounding theory that "every patient conceals a narrative, [their] pathogenic secret." Young suggested that the primary goal for individuals to disclose that pathogenic secret determined the fundamental role of therapists working with these clients (as cited by McKinney, 2007). Engaging individuals to move toward speaking the truth about the traumatic event was the central focus within the setting. Giving individuals the space to name varying secrets associated with their trauma offers a collective healing within communities that often suffer from the silence that ensues after specific traumatic events. While the number of children impacted by parental incarceration has grown to six million across the United States (Annie Casey Foundation, 2017), it remains hidden due to the societal responses of criminalizing parents and pathologizing family members of those incarcerated.

The conspiracy of silence is the failure to disclose to a child that a family member is incarcerated. This includes the deception and shading of the truth that are commonly found in families affected by incarceration. Children are taught and encouraged to refer to prison or jail as army camp, a hospital, work, or school. This reinforces the shame associated with having a parent in prison and further complicates feelings of worry, anxiety, fear, anger, and dissociative responses to their missing parent. Lifting the conspiracy of silence for children of incarcerated parents permits the development of security and internalized power that children can embrace and understand as they feel seen and valued within the context of their community. By sharing collectively in a community of other children, along with family members, they are able to lift the feelings of forced silencing in their experiences based on the shame they receive from school settings, community programs, mental health clinics, and religious institutions. Young's work outlined the unpacking of the "trauma story" and naming of unique psychosocial stressors that are traumatic and shared within this community of children (as cited by McKinney, 2007).

For the conspiracy of silence to be broken, the individual experiencing the trauma must tell the story to someone who, through perceptive listening, bears witness to both the trauma of the individual and the traumatic historical event (McKinney,

2007). Clinicians often miss the central traumatic experience of loss when they do not take the necessary steps to understand the collective systemic violence children and their parents endure within the carceral system. "Survivor silence," as defined by Young, is thought to signify only psychological or political repression and the "unspeakability" of traumatic pasts (as cited by McKinney, 2007). Parents perpetuate this societal and systemic silencing when they feel forced to make up stories about where their child's parent is in an effort to protect them from the vicious cycle of bullying, labeling, and questioning of one's family values and practices, if this information were to be disclosed. Several parents from Children of Promise, NYC shared their story of silencing in all community-based settings, which continually reinforced the feeling of shame. Naquana,[1] a mother of three children within this program, attends several of the parent groups within the clinical setting and shared openly about how it is common practice to lie about where the child's parent was in an effort to protect them. Naquana shared this example that several of the parents within the long-term group setting confirmed as their experience as well:

> When Tamir was 10 years old, his father was unable to attend Bring Your Parent to School Day. When he was asked where his father was, he told his teacher he was in college. I told him when he was six years old that Daddy went away to college because I was too afraid of the bullying I saw his older brother receive when he shared with his classmates that his father was in jail. I watched my oldest son get into fights with teachers defending his father's name and he was labeled in his school as oppositional defiant because he would defend his father when children teased him about not having a father. He'd say, "I have a father, he's in jail and it's not his fault." I remember his teachers expressing concern to me about my home, inquiring if his father did drugs or asking if I had ever been abused. To assume that his father (who was incarcerated for credit card scams) had hurt me or my son was just disgusting. I watched my son suffer for being honest about where his father was, so I wanted to make sure the same thing did not happen to Tamir. So we agreed as a family to tell Tamir his father was in college. I couldn't risk two of my sons being a target in their school community because of the ignorance and intolerance those teachers had.

Several of Naquana's community group members shared similar examples of how they would intentionally choose narratives of the father or mother of the child being in college, the military, sick in the hospital, or away for work as alternatives to their parents being in jail or prison. The parents expressed feeling "afraid" to tell the child's therapist as several settings would often perpetuate racist beliefs and judgments about the parent's behavior as reasons why the child would follow in the footsteps of the parent. Nicole, a mother of two children in the therapeutic program, described how her children's social worker responded during an intake session when she disclosed to the social worker that her children's father was incarcerated:

> When I wanted my sons to be seen for their emotional responses to their father being gone, I hadn't decided yet if I was going to tell them where he went. During the intake with the therapist, I shared with her that he had been arrested and was looking to do seven to ten years. Without asking how my children or I were doing with this loss, she immediately said, "Wow, ten years? He must have done something awful." I was enraged. I proceeded to tell her that he had been involved in a conspiracy that was still unfounded but was immediately

[1] Pseudonyms are used in this chapter to preserve confidentiality.

> charged because of his relationship to his cousin's involvement in a gang. The therapist continued to say, "But they wouldn't have found him guilty if he didn't do anything, so I imagine they probably had evidence and maybe just didn't tell you the extent of it." I explained to her I was aware of all of the evidence and this country has a legacy of sending innocent people to jail. She continued to interrogate me about my parenting skills, if my children ever saw their father hurt me, if there were drugs in the house since his cousin was in a gang, and her growing concern about how the children may have been impacted by his perceived behavior. All of which I hadn't even had a chance to share. I explained politely that I was looking for services for my children to process the loss of their father and to get help in disclosing to them where he was and how long he would be away. I then said that due to her accusations about the kind of father he is, I would be taking my boys somewhere else. This led me to feel like it wasn't safe for them to tell any adults where he was if I told them the truth.

The group members communicated the overwhelming feeling of fear they felt in sharing with their children due to the lack of knowledge about the causes that have led to mass incarceration. The parents stated that they wanted to protect their children from harms caused by a lack of understanding and awareness from teachers, therapists, community members, or anyone else who could reinforce false narratives to their children.

The narratives of children who have transitioned out of the conspiracy of silence share about what they experienced when they told authoritative figures where their parent was. In an interview at a group therapy session at Children of Promise, NYC, several of the children noted that the first question they are often met with is, "What did your mom/dad do?" Talia, age 14, shared, "No one ever asked me how I felt. When someone's parents get divorced or a parent passes away, they get met with, 'I'm so sorry that happened, how are you holding up?' but when I told my teacher I was not feeling like I could focus in class because my dad was arrested and being held in jail, she said to me, 'What did he do?' As if that matters? That's my father." The group members expressed anger that they did not receive any offerings of empathy or simply were not asked how they felt. They continued to acknowledge how this would lead to insecurity, self-doubt, and fear as they continually denied themselves the opportunity to openly process until they came to a therapeutic setting where people not only understood their pain but also validated the pain of this loss and honored their parents with respect. Only then could a level of healing begin.

The conspiracy of silence for children impacted by parental incarceration is also upheld within the therapeutic community. While it is widely accepted that the everyday lives of people who experience intergenerational trauma embody the "absence of presence" of the past and the absence of descendant knowledge of that past as narratives is more challenging to unpack when a child experiences intentional and protective hiding. Hidden wounds from the conspiracy of silence can be consciously and unconsciously transmitted through parents and their decisions to protect their child's experience from the outside world that, in turn, lacks understanding and honoring of the parent. Without an anti-oppressive and anti-racist framework of clinical work, the conspiracy of silence will continue throughout a therapeutic experience as clinician and their supervisors reinforce harmful beliefs about incarcerated parents. Caitlin, a social worker at a Children of Promise, NYC, shared her experience of speaking with her supervisor after an intake and how she was encouraged to call ACS once the father disclosed that his son's mother was incarcerated:

> I remember feeling overwhelmed when the child's father broke down in our initial session about how his wife would be gone for the next three years of his daughter's life and how afraid he was to raise his daughter on his own. The father explained he had not told his daughter yet as he feared she would begin to act out in school and cause more stress for the family. I assured the father it was normal for him to feel worried about his daughter's behavior and that I would work with him on deciding if and when he felt ready to tell her about her mother if he needed that support. When I later shared my own countertransference of sadness in my supervision session, my supervisor was extremely critical that I didn't ask what the mother did to receive the sentence. I shared with her that I didn't feel that was relevant as the father was able to share how loving and wonderful his wife was and what an amazing mother she was to his daughter. I expressed I felt the clinical relevance of supporting him with a disclosure and creating a safe space for his daughter to process the loss should be the focus. My supervisor continued to express her concern about my inability to assess for "risk" and that if the mother was arrested and incarcerated it was "safe to assume she probably struggled to be a good parent." I remember feeling like I wanted to keep this information to myself to protect the client and recognized how I myself could perpetuate the conspiracy of silence in my own work due to the fear I had of consequences from my supervisor.

When clinicians show a lack of clinical humility as it relates to the conspiracy of silence, they perpetuate systemic and institutional racism through the embodiment of their racial bias and beliefs about individuals who are incarcerated. These harms can be experienced directly by the child or adult in session, as well as the clinician or supervisor, when vocalized in ways that carry assumptions about a child's parent or loved one. This harmful clinical process can cause the client to experience secondary traumatization by participating in the conspiracy of silence. The inability to recognize the child's need to maintain an accountable space to process their own narrative feelings about the loss of their parent further encourages children or parents to remain silent and secretive about a parent being in jail or prison. They join historical as well as current societal responses in denying the truth of carceral violence and the truth of human suffering that is directly linked to the loss of a parent to the prison system. Denying the child's truth about their parent that they love and care for not only harms the child but also harms the incarcerated parent who struggles to feel seen and heard by their family, as their incarceration remains a secret. In this regard, the responsibility of the therapist or clinical supervisor is to bear witness to the family's narrative of painful loss by naming the harm in the lack of acknowledgment or denial by others about what happened and by the inability of the parents to acknowledge or bear witness to their own children's feelings of grief and loss. When children are encouraged to share openly and honestly, the conspiracy of silence becomes lifted, and this disclosure process then becomes the vehicle by which identity can be empowered and newly defined. Clinicians cannot explore how deeply impactful the conspiracy of silence is in hopes to support the family to name truths, without fully and honestly addressing relevant issues that have caused barriers for mental health providers to fully admit their part in the silencing (Subotnik, 2016).

Ambiguous Loss: "My Dad Is Here But He's Not Here"

Ambiguous loss, as researched by Pauline Boss in the late 1970s, refers to conditions in which a family member or loved one is psychologically present and physically absent (e.g., losses due to divorce, foster care, or parental incarceration) or psychologically absent and physically present (e.g., losses due to dementia or mental illness; Boss, 1999). Research suggests that ambiguous loss is a common experience for young children, aged 8–15, in systems that separate children from their parents and caregivers (Lee & Whiting, 2007; Mitchell, 2016; Mitchell & Kuczynski, 2010), which now includes the discussion of parental incarceration.

Ambiguous loss, which is commonly defined as a loss without closure, creates and complicates the grieving process for children of incarcerated parents. This chapter will also explore the implications of this theory on clinical practice and describe two common ambiguous loss types experienced by the children, both of which increase the internalization and externalization of symptoms uniquely expressed and experienced by this population. Lange (2000) demonstrated how children use fantasy and imagination to fill in the gaps of information; they may incorrectly come to the distressing conclusion that their parents' absence is voluntary. At times, children can also attempt to make sense of this loss by developing narratives that they themselves are unloved or to blame for the absence (Mitchell, 2016). Children can even begin forming patterns of mistrust in their own ability to form sustainable connections if their perceived reality does not correspond with adult deception (Mitchell, 2016). If clarity of the absence fails to be maintained or the child starts to sense something is amiss, they may withdraw and become distrustful of both caregivers (Council on Crime and Justice, 2006). These become potentially distressing psychosocial experiences that can result in feelings of traumatic loss, confusion, anxiety, and depression.

Symbolic Loss

Symbolic loss, such as the anticipated losses of a physically absent parent, refers to the child's psychosocial losses (Rando, 1984) associated with the physical loss of that relationship. For example, the loss of a "future with their parent" and the loss of "routine and financial stability" are forms of losses that a child can experience in tandem with physical losses (Mitchell & Kuczynski, 2010). The theory of symbolic loss offers another critical lens through which to unpack the grief and loss that children of incarcerated parents experience. Children of incarcerated parents can experience various types of symbolic and intangible losses, for example, a loss of parental fidelity (Leathers, 2003), a loss of identity (Kools, 1997; Mitchell, 2016), a loss of normalcy (Unrau et al., 2008), and a loss of beliefs (Mitchell, 2016). Rayah, age 16, expressed the emotional experiences of symbolic loss after her mother was incarcerated. Rayah discussed the loss of her routine and growing sense of self. She stated:

> My mom was and still is my best friend. We did everything together. There wasn't anything going on in my life that she didn't know about. Not many of my friends were as close to their moms as I am to mine. When I think about prom, my high school graduation, my college acceptance, my college graduation, my engagement, my mom would have been the only person I wanted at every one of those. To have her gone makes me feel unsure about what those times will even look like and if I even want them anymore. I think about how proud I am to be like her. She calls me her mini-me and so does everyone in my family. To know my best friend and my mentor is gone makes it very hard to feel like I know who I am or how to think about my future.

Similarly, Wayne, age 18, also discusses the loss of identity as a result of losing his father. He reported:

> I did everything my dad did. He was my idol. I played football because he did, I worked at the same restaurant he did, and wanted to go to the same college he did. When he was arrested this last year, I felt like I lost a part of myself. He had been beside me the whole way showing me what to do and how to move through all of these obstacles he had to face. With him gone I now question everything. I feel so angry, confused, and scared about a future I thought I had with him.

As illustrated by these narratives, losing a parent to the carceral system can challenge a youth's sense of self through the lens of shared strengths within their family, their own identity of belonging in the world, and overall hope for their future. This example offers deeper insight into the physical, emotional, and psychological impact of this loss felt by children and older teens. The recognition of every facet impacted by this loss guides clinicians to center the symbolic loss as a primary trauma symptom in the child's treatment.

Disenfranchised Grief

Mitchell (2016) eloquently defined how disenfranchised grief can occur when the loss someone experiences is not acknowledged as significant, the parental relationship is not recognized (e.g., incarceration instead of a death or divorce), the griever is excluded (e.g., a child's "inability" to grieve as parents believe they are "too young"), or if the grieving style is considered socially unacceptable (e.g., a child who displays rage and anger but is labeled as defiant or aggressive). This theory is aligned with the belief that children of incarcerated parents have experiences of ambiguous loss that are not compassionately acknowledged or attended to by the child welfare system or society (Mitchell, 2016; Mitchell & Kuczynski, 2010). The narrative shared by Kamee, a 10-year-old who lost her father to incarceration, demonstrates the experience of disenfranchised grief:

> When my mom told me that my daddy was arrested over the weekend he picks me up for my visit, I was scared and mad. My mom told me that she didn't think I'd understand and didn't want to get into it with me. I'm in fifth grade, I know what's going on, I know what jail is and what the cops do. When I told my teacher at school, she said my daddy must have done something very bad. That made me even more mad. I couldn't show my mom I was

> mad, and I didn't want to get in trouble in school so I couldn't talk back to my teacher when she said that mean thing about my daddy. I didn't know what to do. I was so mad.

Kamee's example highlights the unaddressed pain by trusted adults who have messaged to her she is "too young" to understand and therefore process, as well as not offering the proper empathy as the teacher expressed her own biased beliefs about who her father was without making space for Kamee's grief to be shown through anger.

Mitchell (2016) stated that our broader society, as well as within individual experiences, operates from a "grief-denying society" (p.4). Mitchell continued to convey that a "hierarchy of loss" influences how non-death loss is not as valued or deemed as significant by society (p.4). Examples of this are shown through organizational policies across the country that offer paid leave to employees for bereavement associated with death losses but not to individuals who experience divorce, separation, or the loss of a parent to jail or prison (non-death loss), although all of these events are measured as significant life transitions that can result in grief, depression, isolation, and trauma (Hooyman & Kramer, 2006). Furthermore, the lack of support, empathy, and consideration by the broader society and its position on non-death loss at the macro level influence how children who grieve the loss of their parent to incarceration are impacted at the micro level. The minimizing of this loss further perpetuates the emotional distress that is denied and silenced within children who are unable to publicly grieve the loss of their parent.

Children who experience loss related to parental incarceration are often not afforded the same open and supportive space to grieve as this is regularly disrupted by racially assumptive and implicit bias by the broader society, which leads to the continuum of the conspiracy of silence. Boss (1994) emphasized that the crucial theoretical premise of ambiguous loss is the most stressful loss because it defies resolution and creates confused perceptions about ourselves, our family, and our stability. Boss further posits that a clear or tangible loss such as death, which offers a death certificate or mourning rituals of memorials and funerals, supports and honors opportunities to process that loss. With ambiguous loss, there is no clarity or opportunity to identify meaningful rituals that are recognized by the community at large. This clarity can bring necessary closure and avoid further confusion that can lead to feelings of anxiety, depression, isolation, and low self-worth (Boss, 1994). Individuals who are exposed to sudden and traumatic losses often engage in meaning-making to cope with stressful life events (Gan et al., 2013; Lord et al., 2014). Therefore, this next case example illustrates how a child and their parent participated in joint therapeutic sessions at Children of Promise, NYC to work toward both a healing disclosure and the development of rituals to honor the loss of the child's father, to make meaning out of his physical loss and preserve the significance of his psychological and emotional presence for the child.

Case Study: Lifting the Conspiracy of Silence and Making Meaning with Ambiguous Loss

The following case study is an example of a local deployment of a joint caregiver-child intervention designed to facilitate the disclosure process in an effort to minimize adversity while ensuring maximal positivity for both parties, as well as bolstering understanding of incarceration to combat the stigmatization associated with this form of loss. This case study discusses the associations between the conspiracy of silence, ambiguous loss, and the development of trauma-related symptomatology that are addressed through a therapeutic disclosure process. The treatment conditions addressed through the therapeutic process of disclosure and meaning-making establish initial outcomes from treatment as well as the implications for utilizing disclosure and meaning-making framed by addressing ambiguous loss as a utility for children affected by parental incarceration.

Presenting Problem: Case Conceptualization

Theresa, a 33-year-old woman, sought mental health services for her 12-year-old daughter, Kani. During an initial telephone screening with the clinician, Theresa explained that her husband, Stephen, was incarcerated at a New York State correctional facility and had been referred to the clinic because of its mission to work with children and families affected by incarceration. Theresa came in for her initial intake session with her daughter and shared relevant information about their relationship and the closeness they both have with her husband, Kani's father. The initial session Theresa had with the clinician by herself and then the following sessions were designed by Theresa and the clinician for the disclosure process that Kani would be able to experience with her mother and therapist. Over the course of the next month, there would be four disclosure sessions scheduled prior to long-term therapeutic support. The initial session would be the intake to gather background and relevant information regarding the present experience for the family, the second session would be with the child to identify their current thoughts and feelings associated to separation, the third session would be with the social worker and parent to prepare the parent for any emotional experiences they may have or for what specific information they feel comfortable sharing with the child, and the fourth session would be with the child and parent for full disclosure. The structure is designed to support both the parent and the child as well as the incarcerated loved one to all share the same information, lift the conspiracy of silence within the home or among the family members, and provide crucial information for the child to avoid psychosocial stressors associated with ambiguous loss. It is critical to note that, while the disclosure stage is four sessions, long-term therapeutic care will continue once the process of sharing the information about the parent is completed.

Initial Intake

During the first in-person session, the social worker asked Theresa to share the story about her relationship to her family, the night of the arrest, and the stressors she is presently facing. The intention of both the mother and daughter identifying their own relationships to the incarcerated loved one is to combat the experiences many families have in mental health settings where the incarcerated loved one is often criminalized. This process of utilizing clinical narrative and relationship tools to guide the sharing process permits the family to feel seen and heard within their own lived experiences and relationship to the traumatic loss.

Theresa opened the session by stating she had been with her husband for over 15 years, as they met in high school. Kani shared openly about the closeness she had to her father and the desire to better understand where he was and how long he would be gone. On the night of the arrest that led to Stephen's incarceration, Kani had been at her friend's house for a sleepover and Theresa witnessed the arrest on the street as they were walking home from dinner for their weekly date night. Theresa saw the police rush upon Stephen, throw him to the ground, beat him, and then put him in their car without answering any of the questions that Theresa was screaming as they took her husband away.

While her husband was detained, she called the mother of Kani's friend to confirm she would be able to stay another evening with them. She shared that she was "too afraid to tell her what happened and needed more time to understand what my story would be." Theresa reported that over the next few days, she was unable to sleep or focus and was terrified to tell Kani what had happened. Theresa explained that she did not want Kani to worry, and she decided to tell her that he had to pay his family an emergency visit because he had an unwell family member. Theresa admitted that she was still struggling with the emotional effects of witnessing the physical assault and victimization of her husband and, after seeing a therapist, had been diagnosed with complex PTSD.

Theresa received feedback from her family members that she should not share with Kani about where her father was for fear that she would be "made fun of, embarrassed, or shamed." Theresa expressed that it was difficult to share openly with friends as her husband had an outstanding reputation in their community and she was protective of his image. When she recognized how the following 2 weeks brought additional stress due to her hiding the truth from Kani, she knew she needed help from the organization that specialized in this unpacking process for families impacted by this specific trauma. This initial intake was an opportunity for the social worker to help Theresa identify her own personal stressors, pain, and fear, while developing a process by which they could share with Kani with a language that Theresa felt comfortable with. She shared with the social worker that it was essential to uplift Kani's father, allow her to ask any questions, and give her a language she could share with her family and friends. The social worker informed Theresa that within their practice they would have an initial session with Kani to allow for her to share about anything she feels is presently stressful with her father being away and then prepare her for a third session, where the mother and social worker would support Kani through the disclosure process. The session concluded with the social worker structuring ongoing individual sessions for Kani post-disclosure and then ongoing joint family sessions with Kani and Theresa after the disclosure. Theresa agreed to this therapeutic structure and thanked the social worker repeatedly as she cried about no longer feeling alone.

Pre-disclosure Session with Child

The social worker met with Kani to discuss her feelings about her father being away for the past 4 weeks. The social worker wanted to make space for Kani to speak to the physical adjustment on her own and share any pertinent information about his transition. During the first section of the session, the social worker asked her to describe her relationship with her father. The social worker had been trained in both the conspiracy of silence and ambiguous loss theories of practice that the relationship described by the child was central to her own narrative and by necessity would be taking up the most space in the therapeutic work. Stephen, through the lens of Kani, would be amplified throughout their therapeutic work together. Kani described Stephen as being "loving, kind, thoughtful, always supports me and my mom, and he's really smart and funny." Kani became tearful when sharing that she was confused as to why he had left to take care of another family member who "was sick" when "he has his family here to take care of, me and my mom." The social worker expressed appreciation for learning all the warm feelings Kani had about her father and validated her confusion about his not being in the home right now. Kani then shared that she "knew it was probably something else going on, I'm not dumb, but I act like I don't know because I know it makes my mom feel better." The social worker inquired further about what she may feel is happening with her father and she shared, "I don't exactly know, but it's clear that it's not my family he's taking care of, otherwise, I would be able to talk to him more. My mom puts me on the phone with him quickly and he sounds scared. Then she rushes me off and he doesn't get to tell me how he's really doing. I know it's something else." The session concluded with Kani and the social worker agreeing to meet with Theresa for their next session and discussing further about the loss of her father, the information she wanted to know, and always creating space to speak lovingly about him as Kani's lived experience with her father is one of great pride and admiration in her life.

Pre-disclosure Session with Parent

The social worker met with Theresa and shared Kani's feedback in her session regarding the recognition that there was "something else going on" with her father. Having extensive clinical experience with children's pre-disclosure process, she normalized this response and shared with Theresa that it was "very common for children to already have an understanding that their parent is not where the other parent says they are." The social worker provided psychoeducation regarding children's intuitive skill set and the power of the relational process with their incarcerated loved one as a guide to recognizing something was distressing about how their parent was effectively engaging with them. In addition, she shared that Kani could sense her father's worry and fear and felt it was very appropriate to be sharing with her during a time when she senses there is something else happening. The social worker continued to share about the conspiracy of silence and how this impacts anxiety, fear, and stress through a lens of ambiguous loss. She also noted that sharing whatever information felt most comfortable to Theresa would strengthen Kani's understanding and internal emotional stability with the knowledge that she can now better understand. Theresa expressed relief that her daughter already knew he was not with family and expressed her appreciation for the social worker continually calling Stephen by name and honoring that "that is her father, regardless of where he is, he's central to our family and will remain that way in our eyes until he is home." She proceeded to share about the abuse he has endured while incarcerated and the shame and stigma she feels when people talk about "criminals" as less than human. The social worker and Theresa closed the session by identifying the information that felt the most important for her to share with Kani during their disclosure session, at which time Theresa expressed her gratitude for "being made to feel safe and like my family is being seen in this painful process."

Disclosure Session

Kani and Theresa met with the social worker for a 90-minute disclosure session. The purpose of the session was to allow for both Theresa and Kani to express their shared experiences of the loss of Stephen, for Theresa to name where he had gone the night of his arrest, and for Kani to have space to ask any questions she felt were necessary to her understanding his absence. The session would close with a continuity of care plan and introduce the nature of long-term therapeutic support in ways that felt the most useful and supportive to the family.

During the start of the session, Theresa became tearful and immediately apologetic toward Kani about "not sharing sooner" in regard to her father's incarceration. She opened with the statement that she was afraid it "would have been too much" for her to accept and wanted Kani to understand that it was not intentional as they normally never kept anything from each other. As Theresa described the arrest, where Stephen had gone, and the length of time he would be there, the tears welled up in Kani's eyes. She took her mother's hand and began to tell her "it [was] going to be all right" and that "he [was] a fighter." The social worker supported the nurturing tendencies that both Theresa and Kani were displaying toward one another as they moved closer during the disclosure and Kani was able to share that she "understood it was hard to tell me" because of "what people would think." Kani was told she would be able to "ask any questions she wanted," to which she responded by inquiring about her father's arrest, his trial, and how long he would be gone. Kani expressed a desire to visit her father and felt that they would be able to speak more freely since she "knew everything now." Kani was able to openly express that she felt she "knew something was going on" but "was not angry" with her mother, "just the rest of the world for making this so hard to talk about." The session concluded with the family agreeing to ongoing individual and family psychotherapy, as well as phone calls with Stephen during their session, as they work on collective healing as a family.

Ongoing Clinical Care

Over four 90-minute disclosure sessions, the clinical team administered a comprehensive biopsychosocial assessment, trauma assessment, adult trauma checklist, and psychiatric evaluations to identify any ongoing chronic traumatic stress and symptoms experienced by both Theresa and Kani, who expressed feelings of anxiety and worry. A clinical treatment plan was established for both individuals, recommending that Theresa and Kani would each be seen once weekly for individual psychotherapy. The treatment plan also recommended that the family receive joint sessions on a bi-weekly basis over the course of the time Stephen was incarcerated. The model was described in further detail to the family as consisting of the following three phases: (1) the disclosure phase, which they had completed; (2) the narrative phase, to lift the conspiracy of silence in both of their lives; and (3) the meaning-making phase, which would allow for Kani to develop her own rituals and practices honoring this physical loss that she had been unable to do during her father's arrest and incarceration. The phases of this model address both the conspiracy of silence and the ambiguous loss experienced by all family members.

Reflection Questions

1. What is the difference between Conspiracy of Silence and Ambiguous Loss?
2. What social and emotional factors impact reasons for parents or caregivers to choose not to disclose to their children where the incarcerated parents are?
3. As a clinician working with a child impacted by parental loss due to incarceration, what do you feel would be the most challenging in addressing ambiguous loss?
4. How would you clinically describe the difference between symbolic loss and disenfranchised grief?

References

Annie Casey Foundation. (2017). *Kids Count Data Book*. Baltimore, MD.

Arditti, J. A. (2012). Families and incarceration: An ecological approach. *Families in Society, 86*(2), 251–260.

Boss, P. (1994). Ambiguous loss. In F. Walsh, & M. McGoldrick (Eds.), *Living beyond loss: Death in the family* (pp. 237–246). W.W. Norton & Company.

Boss, P. (1999). *Ambiguous Loss: Learning to Live with Unresolved Grief*. Harvard University Press.

Boss, P. (2007). Ambiguous loss theory: Challenges for scholars and practitioners. *Family Relations, 56*(2), 105–110.

Chui, W. H. (2016). Incarceration and family stress as understood through the family process theory: Evidence from Hong Kong. *Frontiers in Psychology, 7*, 881.

Council on Crime and Justice. 2006. *Children of incarcerated parents Minneapolis, MN: Author*. Retrieved from http://www.crimeandjustice.org/researchReports/CCJ%20CIP%20FINAL%20REPORT%20updated%201.30.08.pdf

Dallaire, D. H., Ciccone, A., & Wilson, L. C. (2010). Teachers' experiences with and expectations of children with incarcerated parents. *Journal of Applied Developmental Psychology, 31*(4), 281–290.

Gan, Y., Guo, M., & Tong, J. (2013). The role of meaning-focused coping in significant loss. *Anxiety, Stress & Coping, 26*(1), 87–102.

Hairston, C. F. (2003). *Focus on children with incarcerated parents: An overview of the research literature*. W.W. Norton & Company.

Hooyman, N. R., & Kramer, B. J. (2006). *Living through loss: Interventions across the life span*. Columbia University Press.

Johnston, D. (1995). Effects of parental incarceration. In K. Gabel, & D. Johnston (Eds.), *Children of incarcerated parents* (pp. 59–88). Lexington Books.

Kampfner, C. J. (1995). Post-traumatic stress reactions in children of imprisoned mothers. Children of Incarcerated Parents, 89-100.

Kools, S. M. (1997). Adolescent identity development in foster care. *Family Relations, 46*, 263–271.

Krupat, T. (2007). Invisibility and children's rights: The consequences of parental incarceration. *Women's Rights Law Reporter, 29*, 39–43.

Lange, S. M. (2000). The challenges confronting children of incarcerated parents. *Journal of Family Psychotherapy, 11*(4), 61–68.

Leathers, S. J. (2003). Parental visiting, conflicting allegiances, and emotional and behavioral problems among foster children. *Family Relations, 52*(1), 53–63.

Lee, R. E., & Whiting, J. B. (2007). Foster children's expressions of ambiguous loss. *The American Journal of Family Therapy, 35*(5), 417–428.

Lord, J. M., Midwinter, M. J., Chen, Y. F., Belli, A., Brohi, K., Kovacs, E. J., et al. (2014). The systemic immune response to trauma: An overview of pathophysiology and treatment. *The Lancet, 384*(9952), 1455–1465.

McKinney, K. (2007). "Breaking the conspiracy of silence": Testimony, traumatic memory, and psychotherapy with survivors of political violence. *Ethos, 35*(3), 265–299.

Mitchell, M. (2016). The family dance: Ambiguous loss, meaning making, and the psychological family in foster care. *Journal of Family Theory & Review, 8*(3), 360–372.

Mitchell, M. B., & Kuczynski, L. (2010). Does anyone know what is going on? Examining children's lived experience of the transition into foster care. *Children and Youth Services Review, 32*(3), 437–444.

Parke, R., & Clarke-Stewart, K. A. (2001, January). *Effects of parental incarceration on young children*. In National Policy Conference. From prison to home: The effect of incarceration and reentry on children, families, and communities.

Rando, T. A. (1984). *Grief, dying, and death: Clinical interventions for caregivers* (Vol. 2324). Research PressPub.

Simmons, C. W. (2000). Children of incarcerated parents. *CRB note, 7*(2), n2.

Subotnik, D. (2016). *Race talk and the conspiracy of silence: Understanding and facilitating difficult dialogues on race, by Derald wing sue*. Wiley. 2015, 304pp., $55.00 hardbound, $29.95 paperback. *Academic Questions, 29*(3), 356–362.

Unrau, Y. A., Seita, J. R., & Putney, K. S. (2008). Former foster youth remember multiple placement moves: A journey of loss and hope. *Children and Youth Services Review, 30*(11), 1256–1266.

Part II
Clinical Applications Grounded in Cultural Responsiveness

Chapter 4
Narrative Therapy

The clinician's understanding of a shared humanity is a prerequisite for the clinical relationship. Many of the clients seen by clinical social workers have challenges tolerating and managing difficult feelings and affective states. Narrative practices shift a clinician's position to "helpers" and make the child the expert in their own life as they begin to share their own lived experience in regard to the loss of their parent(s) to the criminal justice system. It is no longer a requirement to be the expert on another's life. The emphasis in narrative therapy is on understanding and meaning. The clinician aims to better understand the individual's reality within their social and cultural context. In the process of deconstruction through narrative, individuals begin to see their identity as something separate from the problem: The problem becomes the problem. Alternate stories about the nature of individuals and society can be revealed when someone has autonomy over their own narrative. When given space to share their story, individuals can make meaning of their own experience, and clinicians are given the opportunity to better understand the individual on their own terms, in their own words, and from their own perspective.

For children of incarcerated parents, who are commonly encouraged to hide their painful experience of loss, narrative therapy is an essential and effective tool. Throughout this chapter, shared excerpts from participants engaged in this model will signify how children impacted by parental incarceration identify the changes they experience.

Narrative therapy asserts that our beliefs, challenges, and qualities are all products of culture and history (Castan, 2020) and that identity is created in relationship and community with others, rather than expressing something "core" and "internal" (Carey & Russell, 2004). Narrative therapy is best known for its practices of externalizing problems encountered in practice with children and supporting the transitional process which removes the identity the child has of the problem and therefore can impact their primary sense of self (Freeman et al., 1997).

A. Morgan-Mullane, *An Integrative Approach to Clinical Social Work Practice with Children of Incarcerated Parents*, Essential Clinical Social Work Series,
https://doi.org/10.1007/978-3-031-28823-4_4

Children of incarcerated parents experience feelings of depression and anxiety, which are more commonly expressed through an internalization process within their varying stages of development. While many clinicians consider depression and anxiety as two separate disorders, comorbidity can often occur in children of incarcerated parents (Jalali et al., 2019). Depression among children and adolescents can be accompanied by severe symptoms of anxiety (Angold et al., 1999; Cummings et al., 2014; Garber & Weersing, 2010). Many children who have experienced an abrupt loss of a parent to the prison system share about suffering from overwhelming thoughts of worry or fear associated with their parent. This can be commonly experienced throughout their school day, further exacerbating disruption to their learning process. Anxiety disorder is one of the most common disorders among children that leads to disruption in academic performance, social adjustment, family life, and relationships with peers (Warner et al., 2009). The pervasiveness of depression among children is estimated at approximately 2% (Costello et al., 2003). Depression can heighten significant challenges to children's social and emotional functioning, which can include a decrease in energy to perform impactfully in their academic settings and difficulty in relationships with peers and family (Weisz et al., 2006).

Among children with imprisoned parents, narrative individual and group psychotherapy modalities are more likely to result in a greater reduction of anxiety symptoms as children are offered the opportunity to share their own story in their individual therapy and find shared communal experiences in group-based activities. Similarly, with children who have internalized feelings of depression, both narrative group and individual therapy are more likely to result in a greater reduction of depression symptoms as children embrace an increase of internal power by feeling inspired in their own stories and the meaning-making of the traumatic event as their primary lived experience. Children have a difficult time expressing their feelings and emotions in a precise manner as their level of abstract thinking is still developing (Dumontheil, 2014) and, therefore, benefit from therapeutic interventions such as narrative storytelling and play therapy. Play therapy, frequently used throughout narrative therapy, is a clinical tool that facilitates authentic self-expression (Bratton et al., 2005) when the child is addressing suppressed feelings and difficult memories. Narrative therapy for children is a type of play therapy (Arad, 2004), and this methodology is regularly used as a central standpoint within the practice of child and family therapy. Through variations in language and literature of one's own life story, narrative therapy establishes a creative opportunity for relationship and behavior with others (DeSocio, 2005).

Two examples of narrative therapy are offered within the case examples from CPNYC. As the social workers within this organization employ anti-racist and anti-oppressive lenses in their clinical work, narrative therapies focus specifically on the children's and families' own story and rely on narratives and stories to help the children to make new meaning about who they are, who they have been, and who they want to be (Prochaska & Norcross, 2018). This is in juxtaposition to clinical practices that can place blame on the individual and pathologize trauma symptoms that are normal expressions of anxiety, fear, and sadness as they relate to grieving the loss of a parent to the carceral system. In the narrative group psychotherapy session, the following phases were employed by the clinicians, based on eight essential values of narrative therapy adopted by Michael White (2007): (1) adopt a collaborative co-authoring consultative position; (2) partner with the child and group members to view themselves as separate from their problems by externalizing the problem; (3) support the child/group members to identify times in their lives when they were not distressed by their problems by finding unique outcomes; (4) bolster the child/group members' descriptions of these constructive and empowering outcomes by reshaping action and landscape-of-consciousness questions; (5) connect unique outcomes to other events in the past and extend the story into the future to form an alternative and desired self-narrative in which the self is viewed as more powerful than the problem; (6) invite significant members of the person's social network to witness this new self-narrative; (7) document new knowledge and practices that support the new self-narrative using literary means; and (8) share with others who are fighting similar oppressive narratives who can benefit from their new knowledge (Carr, 1998).

The narrative therapy sessions were implemented every week for 90 minutes in the agency's group psychotherapy teen room. The narratives were developed based on symptoms of depression and anxiety expressed by the children in sessions prior to the narrative group therapy intervention. The clinicians explained that the purpose of the stories was to strengthen individual power and allow for shared attention and collective learning among the children in the group. The common themes for all stories shared by the group members included improving self-concept, processing anger and rage, opportunities to connect with friends, and keeping friendships that would decrease loneliness and help them overcome anxiety and depression. A summary of the therapy sessions is presented in the outline of each phase.

Group Narrative Therapy Case Illustration: Teen Trauma-Based Healing Group

The teen trauma-responsive psychotherapy group at Children of Promise, NYC meets once a week for 90 minutes to focus on a new theme each treatment cycle. Over a 4-month period, the children engaged weekly in psychotherapy group sessions to address shared symptoms associated with traumatic loss, which include anxiety, depression, low self-worth, loneliness, isolation, and grief. For this 18-session narrative therapy group model, each student identified their levels of anxiety and sadness by completing the GAD-7 (Generalized Anxiety Disorder-7) self-administered and automatic scoring assessment tool as well as SCARED (Screening for Childhood Anxiety Related Disorders). Each assessment tool allowed for the children to self-measure the weight of their own symptoms and would then be scored again at the end of the 18 sessions. Each participant had one parent presently incarcerated, and all children also engaged in their own individual psychotherapy sessions outside of the group sessions.

1. ***Adopt a Collaborative Co-authoring Consultative Position***

Narrative therapy is a collaborative process providing a space in which any stories of difficulty can be amplified and honored. Narrative therapy also allows for the individual to begin at an entry point to previously unspoken and unproblematic chapters of their life more in keeping with their preferred identity (McQueen & Hobbs, 2014). In the initial group structuring, the teen participants were asked to collaborate on the theme of their universal story. The members also agreed on a common description of the rules of group therapy sessions, establishing a relationship between all participants and therapists. Examples of the "rules" included the following: (1) Everyone has a voice to use; (2) only offer supportive feedback; (3) honor everyone's story; (4) let one person talk at a time; and (5) empower each other after each person shares. The main focus of this session was centered on the creation of a sense of authentic and powerful self-worth, which further reduced feelings of inferiority or devaluation of self and amplified strengths the group members could see in one another as authors.

2. ***Partner with the Child and Group Members to View Themselves as Separate from Their Problems by Externalizing the Problem***

The main focus in this session was the establishment of trust between the teen group members and the clinicians as they formulate language for the externalizing problem being shared within the identified story. In the session prior, the group members established the theme of *amplifying their voice to heal their pain*. Through collective effort, each student shared and wrote excerpts of witnessing their parent's arrest, as well as the barriers they faced with visitation attempts. The role of the clinician was to help provide psychoeducation on the trauma and impact that witnessing a parental arrest has on an individual's nervous system. This allowed the participants to name and normalize their feelings of anxiety, stress, and anger as trauma responses and not "reasons we were told we were bad by our teachers." By seeing themselves as separate from the trauma, they expressed feeling increased self-acceptance, caring about helping each other relieve the pain, emphasizing that the beauty is inside and not on the outside, in the ways they responded to the anger. Each student shared about their unique pain of witnessing a parent being arrested, and how they felt that the clinicians provided a healing space for them to share openly about their rage and anxiety without feeling criminalized for it. These shifting narratives were reflected in chapters of their narrative, woven throughout their "Amplifying Our Voice to Heal Our Pain" story.

3. ***Support the Child/Group Members to Identify Times in Their Lives When They Were Not Distressed by Their Problems by Finding Unique Outcomes***

The primary purpose of this session was to emphasize strategies to overcome anxiety and stress by identifying recent experiences where the participants self-identified feeling proud of themselves and did not feel overwhelmed by the loss of a parent. Each student provided examples of what they felt emotionally when they started attending their therapeutic program at the agency. One youth noted, "It was in the sharing of my story in all of my activities here that I began to worry less about my mom and think more about how my story could help someone else." Another teen shared about her ability to communicate with her father who is incarcerated through writing letters at the organization and how cathartic it felt to speak openly in her writing toward him: "It was when I started writing my dad letters in my letter-writing class here that I realized I wasn't alone in my pain, I could share with him what I was going through, and I didn't have to feel like he was so far away. It was like letting out a deep breath." The teens continually provided examples of the outlets they found within their friendships with others who had incarcerated parents that relieved their feelings of worry and fear.

4. ***Bolster the Child/Group Members' Descriptions of These Constructive and Empowering Outcomes by Using Reshaping of Action and Landscape-of-Consciousness Questions***

Within this session, there was an emphasis on each teen's authentic voice and creativity, presenting a pattern for self-confidence, the concept of trust, and training in problem-solving methods (McQueen & Hobbs, 2014). Critical consciousness and reimagining power were encouraged by the clinicians. As students began to narrate their own view of self-transformation, they wrote about their pain of losing their loved one as a voice of power to bring about change in policy. Examples of this were shown through Corey's[1] narrative, which stated, "I began to look at what was happening in the legal system and why they took my dad and gave him the sentence they did. How could he do 10 years for marijuana? Would, could this be just? So I took my pain and turned it into power and began researching." Another teen conveyed how listening to the other group members share their narratives "made me realize that we have a power in our story as being experts in the lives of those affected by this loss. We don't have to see it as something to be ashamed of, but you have all taught me it's my power to talk about how Black and Brown communities are plagued with having our families ripped away from us, and only we can share what the pain really feels like. People can learn from our stories."

5. ***Connect Unique Outcomes to Other Events in the Past and Extend the Story into the Future to Form an Alternative and Desired Self-Narrative in Which the Self Is Viewed as More Powerful Than the Problem***

This session focused on effective communication that was used throughout the previous sessions on the collective sharing of stories of empowerment. Each teen was able to provide a specific example of when they spoke to someone in their school, community, or local government about how children are affected by parental loss from mass incarceration. By highlighting their stories, each student became more enthusiastic about what each group member was saying in their conversations with the broader community. They magnified the shared characteristics about their incarcerated loved ones in their writing, such as "a powerful mother, a strong father,

[1] Pseudonyms are used in this chapter to preserve confidentiality.

a committed brother, a protective sister," which further reflected their newfound belief in and influences on whom they believed themselves to be. Examples of this were conveyed in narratives such as, "I used to see myself as weak and scared, now I see my story makes me powerful. I understand and believe my mother is strong in what she is going through and, therefore, I believe I am strong because I am her daughter." The teen participants reshaped their self-narrative to now include parallel language of admiration for their parents and personal self-love.

6. ***Invite Significant Members of the Person's Social Network to Witness This New Self-Narrative***

The main idea in this session was to underscore the community and trust the group had created in their co-authored writing and collaborative narrative and begin sharing specifically with one another the ways in which they have reimagined their own power. The members shared honestly with one another about their transformation from feeling anxious and overwhelmed by examples such as, "I used to mistrust the world. I thought no one could be trusted after I watched police brutalize my dad, but today I see my story of sharing his pain makes me a leader and I can trust my own story." Another example of narrative emotional transformation shared within the group was a teen who conveyed, "Watching you all begin to retell your story made me feel like it was possible to retell mine. I never thought I had anything worthy to say, everyone said horrible things about my mom being in jail, but listening to you all share that our stories make us powerful made me think maybe I had a light inside of me too." The group sharing offered each member the chance to listen to one another and add additional strengths, as one teen shared after his peer spoke: "Honestly, I know you said you struggled with getting mad, but your anger is real, bro. You deserve to let it out. Stop saying you were a bad kid and now you're not. How about you say you were carrying anger and now you're healing?" The group members' response created a space for the rest of the teens to validate what was exchanged between the two group members as several students and clinicians became emotional in watching the co-created healing moment.

7. ***Document New Knowledge and Practices That Support the New Self-Narrative Using Literary Means***

The principal objective of this group session was to share the story of transformation to expand the group members' recognition of their cognitive and emotional expressions of hope. By instilling hope in one another, the group members gave specific examples of how they no longer felt alone or isolated or acted on their rage or withdrawn behaviors. Several group members gave examples such as, "When you feel your story not only helps you to heal, but helps others to heal, you don't feel so alone." Another participant expressed that "I now know and believe that I'm capable of anything. I feel like I don't have to fight other people when they talk about my dad because I know I'm unique and I probably know more about how messed up the legal system is than they do." All of these illustrations of cognitive beliefs and emotional responses were documented within their group narrative.

8. ***Share with Others Who Are Fighting Similar Oppressive Narratives Who Can Benefit from Their New Knowledge***

The final phase of this group narrative therapy intervention is to allow the group members to read the final version of their story and identify community spaces where they hope to continue to carry out their message. Prior to reading the narrative, the clinicians provided their own observations of how profound the social and emotional growth was in each group member and provided specific examples of how each group member was transformed and offered compassionate support to one another. Mirroring the growth that the clinicians had recognized, the group members were inspired to share with each other what they noticed had been transformed in this narrative process. Several participants shared their narrative pieces and the heroic feelings of joy, excitement, power, pain, depression, sadness, anxiety, and togetherness of the common story developed by everyone in different situations. At the end of this session, the group members expressed a desire not only to share their stories with their incarcerated parents by mailing them copies but also to read them in front of their loved ones that were at home. They decided they wanted to perform them at a local community program in an effort to bring more awareness to the impact of parental incarceration on children and ultimately, "Amplify Our Voice to Heal Our Pain."

Storytelling becomes a way for children to induce feelings of hope (McQueen & Hobbs, 2014). As part of instilling hope, the participants in the narrative group therapy sessions share experiences of a reduction in sadness and loneliness, as well as increased relaxation, catharsis, and a sense of value or self-esteem. By creating a group space where shared identities, relating to feelings and connecting to a safe community, the teen participants develop the concept of confidence and trust. As they experience attachment for the first time in a family (Crittenden & Dallos, 2009), many children of incarcerated parents share how feelings of mistrust commonly develop when the parent is taken away. Therefore, the sense of community that is created in narrative therapy in a group setting offers children the opportunity to heal the mistrust in the world around them and strengthen their feelings of "chosen family" with those they feel most closely connected to. Much of the negative self-talk diminishes as they begin to form healthy bonds and attachments to one another. Furthermore, the group members convey their own strengthened belief in the social relationship among the group and how it invited each participant to create a new and meaningful relationship, capable of helping them to overcome a fear of being in the group and refining incompatible social cognition (McQueen & Hobbs, 2014).

For the purposes of this therapeutic model, group therapy had several benefits for children with imprisoned parents, such as in the context of group communication and identification with other teens who had similar challenges and barriers to their emotional expression as well as overall feelings of depression and anxiety. Group therapy presented a supportive environment for each teen to self-assess the reduction of feeling withdrawn and alone, which is a common experience for children of incarcerated parents. This collective narrative process made it possible for each group member to witness the external healing, allowing each participant to facilitate their own learning process of how they choose to cope with their pain and anger. By witnessing the process of transformation in the meaning of their trauma, group members shared how attainable it felt hearing change from other teens who experienced their "exact story." When the teens provided each other with direct feedback, they shared that they "could hear it more honestly because I knew they had gone through what I went through, so I believed them when they told me change was possible, because they walked through it too."

The second most common clinical modality of narrative therapy used with children of incarcerated parents within an individual psychotherapy capacity is a modification of the STAIR narrative therapy practice model (Cloitre et al., 2006). STAIR refers to assisting individuals to identify and implement Skills Training in Affect and Interpersonal Regulation through a narrative-based approach. This is a phase-based manualized cognitive-behavioral therapy originally developed for PTSD related to childhood abuse, in which skills training precedes trauma narration (Landes et al., 2013). While it can be implemented as an individual or a group modality, the clinicians at Children of Promise, NYC employ a modified version of this intervention in their individual therapeutic sessions with children. The rationale for the development of the treatment modality in the STAIR framework was to reduce PTSD symptoms by employing traditional trauma memory processing as well as concentrating on several challenges reported among people who struggle with PTSD from childhood trauma. The two particular realms of intrusive emotional experiences, specifically emotional regulation challenges and interpersonal disturbances (Landes et al., 2013), were primarily reported as the most significant barriers to healing from trauma. It was supported by the developmental theory that named emotion regulation and relational capacities as core developmental tasks of early life and an empirical literature that demonstrated the disruptive effect of trauma on these functions (Landes et al., 2013). Therefore, the treatment sequence is organized for participants in the model with coping skills, first, to immediately address the challenges in day-to-day functioning and second, to offer the client skills that would allow the more effective use of exposure therapy or play therapy. STAIR narrative therapy comprises a total of sixteen 60-minute individual sessions (16 hours of treatment), which the clinicians at Children of Promise, NYC extended to a longer practice as they wanted to offer clients an extended engagement period to strengthen trust and rapport.

The first phase of treatment consists of eight sessions of practice in emotion regulation and interpersonal skills (Landes et al., 2013). The second phase embodies eight sessions of ongoing skills training with the addition of a modified version of prolonged imaginal exposure for trauma therapy. This model normally utilizes a total of sixteen 60-minute individual sessions. However, the clinicians intentionally allow the children to narratively express their feelings at their own pace, as many have expressed negative experiences in mental health clinics with providers who had rushed their therapeutic experiences and caused increased mistrust within the therapeutic relationship.

The following case illustration is an example of an implementation of the STAIR narrative therapy model and practice designed to facilitate the meaning-making of past and current traumatic symptoms associated with parental loss due to mass incarceration. The process signifies an effort to minimize the child's emotionally taxing experience of their own mistrust with adults while ensuring utmost positivity for both caregiver and child. This example encourages the use of narrative therapy as a profound tool for supporting the child's own understanding of incarceration to combat stigmatization associated with this form of loss.

This case example considers the child's desired growth and change in how they see their primary trauma and offers a healing lens of making meaning out of the recent loss the child experienced in a way that helps them regulate their own emotions. The treatment conditions addressed through the therapeutic process of narrative therapy and meaning-making establish initial outcomes from treatment, as well as the implications for employing this model for effective outcomes of increased emotional awareness and regulation.

Case Illustration: Dylan's Story

Emotional Awareness: Intake Session

At the start of the first session, Dylan, a 10-year-old boy, was first seen by the social worker after his mother researched clinical settings that worked with children of incarcerated parents. During the intake session, Dylan's mother, Sue, provided background on Dylan's current experiences at school in which she described him as "very intelligent, but emotionally shut down after his father has been incarcerated." Sue shared that he was normally very expressive and earned high marks in school but had become more detached from his work, and she was worried about his depression.

Dylan shared openly in the initial session that he felt "responsible" for his father's arrest and was "confused as to why he left." Sue explained she had repeatedly shared that his arrest "had nothing to do with Dylan, but he is trying to make sense of it all and has just become shut down." The social worker praised the family for speaking openly about the father's incarceration, the important relationship Dylan has with his father, and the work they would do within the STAIR model over the course of the next several sessions. The social worker outlined that within the first phase of the model, they would help Dylan focus on his emotional awareness so that he could find new language to express himself and not feel so withdrawn or isolated. The purpose of this phase would be to aid Dylan in learning more about the connection of the traumatic loss of his father and the difficulty he has had finding emotional language to express how he feels. The family closed the session with an overview of the two portions of the framework for the model and that their work would conclude with Dylan's own biography that he would be able to share with his mother. Dylan was excited by the idea of "writing my own story," and his mother felt it was an appropriate intervention as he "is so expressive, but has just been so shut down."

Emotional Regulation

During these sessions, Dylan and the social worker built a rapport and employed several play-based activities that would help Dylan learn how to monitor his feelings, triggers, and thoughts. Dylan would draw pictures and write out sections of his biography of specific instances at home and at school that he felt frustrated by after his father's arrest. Dylan was able to identify triggers when people would ask him why his dad "wasn't around" and "where he was." Dylan acknowledged that he would become "angry and mad" and would "ignore people or just not talk to them." Dylan and his clinician worked on writing out new thoughts and reactions he could have when asked about his father that offered more of a helpful narrative as to who he believed his dad to be and to not feel ashamed or mad when someone asked about him. Dylan appreciated this exercise and said he would "try it at school when the kids or teachers ask. I'm proud of who my dad is. I don't want to hide that."

Understanding Relationship Patterns

For this section of the therapeutic model, Dylan and his clinician worked on his own understanding of what ways (e.g., schemas) the traumatic loss of his father influenced his view of himself and his expectations in the world. Dylan would draw pictures about who he felt he was with his father at home, which included narratives of, "I was happy with my dad, I felt safe with my dad," and was able to recognize that with his father gone, he no longer felt safe. The clinician supported the development of reframing the loss to include his father's emotional and psychological impact on Dylan, which continues in their ongoing communication while he is incarcerated. Dylan began writing a chapter that conveyed, "I'm still strong and smart even though my dad isn't here, because my dad is strong and smart even though I'm not with him." Dylan stated that he liked these narrative exercises, as he was able to "feel closer to my dad when I see that we are the same, still."

Improving Interpersonal Relationships in the Here and Now

Dylan self-identified that he became less social with his peers, less engaged with his teachers, and often did not tell his mom how he was feeling. He explained, "When I was nine and my dad was home, I had a lot of friends, I always talked to my teachers, and my mom didn't bother me like she bothers me now." He was able to unpack his own change in behavior after his dad was arrested and how this made him feel less safe or "happy in the world." Dylan was able to learn through this phase how he could draw upon those old patterns of interpersonal relationships from the past and bring them into the present. He was able to practice exercises that offered him new ways of relating and behaving with others, such as his peers, teachers, and mother through activities like role-playing, which demonstrated new skills, such as assertiveness and flexibility/adaptability in interpersonal interactions.

Identifying Current Difficulties as Based in Past Traumas and Letting Them Go

Throughout these sessions in Dylan's narrative, the specific trauma memories he felt were the most painful. These included coming home from school and finding out his father had been arrested, seeing his father on the news, and going to visit him for the first time in jail. Dylan was asked to narratively formulate what specific interpersonal schemas (beliefs, feelings, and behaviors) he experienced during this time and he shared examples such as, "I thought it was my fault since I had gotten in trouble at school that day" or "When I saw him in the news I thought he had been killed" and, finally, "When I went to visit him in jail, I was mad at the people who worked there for hurting him." The clinician normalized these patterns of thinking he had and shared that many of his fears were rooted in truthful events. Dylan and his therapist identified the specific feelings he had such as worry, anxiety, fear, and anger and how he had acted at home and in school as a result of efforts to respond effectively to the traumatic experience he had. The clinician helped to normalize all his feelings and praised him for starting to identify them so accurately when he had been unable to do so before. The clinician and Dylan then addressed how these emotional responses to the people around him had become habits of feeling, thinking, and acting that may no longer be helpful, such as not spending time with friends, withdrawing in class, or ignoring his mother.

This phase of the work concluded with the clinician highlighting the value of these schemas in past situations while presenting options for new ways of feeling and relating to those he cared about through new identification of feelings and role-playing this practice. Dylan was able to acknowledge that he "loved learning" and "seeing [his] friends" and that he "wanted to be able to do that again."

Building an Autobiography: Putting It All Together

To close the STAIR model, Dylan and his clinician put together his final story that he wanted to read aloud to his mother. Dylan was able to organize his narrative to specifically outline the traumatic memories he disclosed throughout the sessions.

He wanted to speak about the day he came home from school to find out that his father would not be home for 10 years. Dylan wrote a chapter on when he saw his father on the news and that he had been "scared for his life and mine." The narrative offers a structure of a beginning, middle, and end to imagine these memories as part of an autobiography. Dylan wrote about visiting his father in jail and the bus ride to see him, how the prison felt, the fear he had of the police, and the anger he felt leaving, knowing his father could not come home with him. Dylan was encouraged to write a chapter on who he was when his father was home, the experiences he had when the family was together, and what he will get to experience with his father when he returns home after the 10 years. The analogy to the autobiography was used to encourage consideration of the traumatic experiences as only some of the many chapters of Dylan's life from which some meaning can be made and used to build a future. The emphasis on Dylan's father throughout each chapter supported Dylan's overarching belief that he "loves [his] dad" and that he "just [wants] him home and safe." Dylan closed the autobiography by sharing what he will do with his father when he is 20 years old, the places he wants to take him, the dreams he hopes to share with him, and that "being a family again is all that matters."

Dylan expressed feeling happy when he finished his story and read it to his mother in his final session. Sue was tearful throughout the reading of Dylan's story as she shared, "He has not expressed himself like this in the last year. It's the first time I'm seeing him back to himself." The clinician was able to use their trusting relationship to encourage Dylan's imagination, writing style, artwork, and self-expression as he began to identify his feelings. Dylan and the clinician continued to see each other for therapeutic sessions throughout the course of the school year to monitor his progress within his classroom setting, his new engagement with his peers, and his comfort in expressing himself more openly at home.

Reflection Questions

1. What are the primary tenants of Narrative Therapy and how does this specific model allow for children to feel less silenced?
2. What specific trauma symptoms does narrative therapy address?
3. How would you describe the differences in application with an individual client versus a client group?
4. Do you feel it would be challenging to hear narratives that might illicit bias in one's story? What tools can you utilize to address this bias and ensure the narrative script remains as honest as possible for the client?
5. Describe your clinical thoughts on co-authoring in narrative therapy?

References

Angold, A., Costello, E. J., & Erkanli, A. (1999). Comorbidity. *The Journal of Child Psychology and Psychiatry and Allied Disciplines, 40*(1), 57–87.

Arad, D. (2004). If your mother were an animal, what animal would she be? Creating play-stories in family therapy: The animal attribution story-telling technique (AASTT). *Family Process, 43*(2), 249–263.

Bratton, S. C., Ray, D., Rhine, T., & Jones, L. (2005). The efficacy of play therapy with children: A meta-analytic review of treatment outcomes. *Professional Psychology: Research and Practice, 36*(4), 376–390.

Carey, M. & Russell, S. (2004). *Narrative therapy: responding to your questions*. Adelaide, S. Aust: Dulwich Centre Publications.

Carr, A. (1998). Michael White's narrative therapy. *Contemporary Family Therapy, 20*(4), 485–503.

Castan, L. (2020). Child-centred play therapy and narrative therapy: Consilience and synthesis. *International Journal of Narrative Therapy & Community Work, 1*, 24–33.

Cloitre, M., Cohen, L. R., & Koenen, K. C. (2006). *Treating survivor of childhood abuse: Psychotherapy for the interrupted life*. Guilford Press.

Costello, E. J., Mustillo, S., Erkanli, A., Keeler, G., & Angold, A. (2003). Prevalence and development of psychiatric disorders in childhood and adolescence. *Archives of General Psychiatry, 60*(8), 837–844.

Crittenden, P. M., & Dallos, R. (2009). All in the family: Integrating attachment and family systems theories. *Clinical Child Psychology and Psychiatry, 14*(3), 389–409.

Cummings, C. M., Caporino, N. E., & Kendall, P. C. (2014). Comorbidity of anxiety and depression in children and adolescents: 20 years after. *Psychological Bulletin, 140*(3), 816.

DeSocio, J. E. (2005). Accessing self-development through narrative approaches in child and adolescent psychotherapy. *Journal of Child and Adolescent Psychiatric Nursing, 18*(2), 53–61.

Dumontheil, I. (2014). Development of abstract thinking during childhood and adolescence: The role of rostrolateral prefrontal cortex. *Developmental Cognitive Neuroscience, 10*, 57–76.

Freeman, J. C., Epston, D., & Lobovits, D. (1997). Playful approaches to serious problems: Narrative therapy with children and their families. WW Norton & Company.

Garber, J., & Weersing, V. R. (2010). Comorbidity of anxiety and depression in youth: Implications for treatment and prevention. *Clinical Psychology: Science and Practice, 17*(4), 293.

Jalali, F., Hasema, S. F., & Hasani, A. (2019). Narrative therapy for depression and anxiety among children with imprisoned parents: A randomised pilot efficacy trial. *Journal of Child & Adolescent Mental Health, 31*(3), 189–200.

Landes, S. J., Garovoy, N. D., & Berkman, K. M. (2013). Treating complex trauma among veterans: Three stage-based treatment models. *Journal of Clinical Psychology, 69*(5), 523–533.

McQueen, C., & Hobbs, C. (2014). Working with parents: Using narrative therapy to work towards genuine partnership. *Educational & Child Psychology, 31*(4), 9–17.

Prochaska, J. O., & Norcross, J. C. (2018). *Systems of psychotherapy: A transtheoretical analysis*. Oxford University Press.

Warner, C. M., Reigada, L. C., Fisher, P. H., Saborsky, A. L., & Benkov, K. J. (2009). CBT for anxiety and associated somatic complaints in pediatric medical settings: An open pilot study. *Journal of Clinical Psychology in Medical Settings, 16*(2), 169–177.

Weisz, J. R., McCarty, C. A., & Valeri, S. M. (2006). Effects of psychotherapy for depression in children and adolescents: A meta-analysis. *Psychological Bulletin, 132*(1), 132–149. https://doi.org/10.1037/0033-2909.132.1.132

White, M. K. (2007). Maps of narrative practice. WW Norton & Company.

Chapter 5
Trauma-Focused Cognitive Behavioral Therapy

This chapter includes an in-depth analysis of the development and utilization of Trauma-Focused Cognitive Behavioral Therapy (TF-CBT) with children of incarcerated parents. This chapter also includes justification for its use in community-based settings, focusing on the versatility and relatively brief treatment term, while describing the assets and limitations of the modality for use with children of incarcerated parents. TF-CBT aims to reduce distress and resolve maladaptive cognition associated with trauma within a brief treatment period of 12–18 sessions. Due to its versatility, TF-CBT became popular for community-based practitioners working in direct service settings with children and adolescents from diverse cultural backgrounds with challenging clinical presentations and complex family situations (Cohen et al., 2006a). With increasing clinical attention given to the emotional distress and complex trauma symptoms experienced by children of incarcerated parents, such as difficulty forming attachments, problems with concentrating and sleeping, inability to develop trust, and difficulty achieving identity (Manning, 2011), this model presently offers a new option to practitioners who work specifically with this population.

In this chapter, the author uses research to present the efficacy and guidelines to employ this therapeutic model. When employed within the agency setting, this model will allow for the child and parent/guardian to quickly engage in a process that safely explores the language and definitions of trauma that begins the healing process necessary to restore the child's ability to function on a day-to-day basis, both at home and at school. The core components used within the model frame the clinical work to empower the child and caregiver to simultaneously learn about their trauma symptoms while effectively mastering the coping mechanisms necessary to manage overwhelming feelings.

A. Morgan-Mullane, *An Integrative Approach to Clinical Social Work Practice with Children of Incarcerated Parents*, Essential Clinical Social Work Series,
https://doi.org/10.1007/978-3-031-28823-4_5

Therapeutically Addressing Parental Incarceration with TF-CBT

Children affected by parental incarceration are typically experiencing complex traumas that are manifested by multiple traumatic and systemic experiences. Commonly, a child with an incarcerated parent will likely have witnessed violent and intrusive interactions with law enforcement officials, including the parent's or loved one's arrest. As a result, the child reports other emotional traumas, such as community police brutality, over-surveillance in their neighborhood, and racial trauma through systemic harm directly caused by mass incarceration. Children experience overlapping, intersectional sources of trauma, and children of incarcerated parents are a highly stigmatized population, which increases self-protection through forms of secrecy, fear, and worry.

Despite the large number of children and families affected by incarceration, limited research has been conducted to explore the effects of parental incarceration on children, as well as what policy interventions exist to mediate the toll exacted upon children and families impacted by the injustice system (Manning, 2011). Existing research implies that parental incarceration is associated with numerous negative effects (Manning, 2011; Miller & Barnes, 2015; Murray et al., 2012; Phillips et al., 2006) and that TF-CBT has the potential to effectively reduce traumatic symptoms associated with parental incarceration. However, a review using the EBSCO database with the search terms "TF-CBT," "parental incarceration," and "children of incarcerated parents" found limited studies or clinical reports indicating that this treatment orientation has been applied to children of incarcerated parents. Because parental incarceration is a complex trauma, secondary traumas (e.g., increased poverty, houselessness) may act as mediating variables for parental incarceration in any TF-CBT applications. Additionally, the methodological difficulties associated with locating a sample of children traumatized by parental incarceration, coupled with issues of secrecy and stigmatization, may explain the research exclusion of this specific group from examining effective treatment interventions (Manning, 2011).

TF-CBT Background

TF-CBT, a more recently developed evidence-based practice, was created and tested by Judith A. Cohen, Anthony P. Mannarino, and Esther Deblinger in the late 1990s and began to receive significant recognition after therapists applied the model to treat individuals who had been affected by the events of September 11, 2001. TF-CBT aims to reduce distress and resolve maladaptive cognitions associated with trauma within a brief treatment period of 12–18 sessions. The first manual was published in 2006 (de Arellano et al., 2014), and the earliest applications of this model to children were by community clinicians who used it to assess and treat traumatic grief in sexually abused children between 3 and 18 years of age.

The first phase of the model begins with trauma psychoeducation for the child to fully understand and normalize the impact of their experience. The second phase consists of gradual exposure, behavior modeling, cognitive coping strategies, and finally, incorporating parent treatment sessions to enhance the child's emotional safety (Erickson et al., 2015). These phases allow the child to regain a sense of security and well-being through the caregiver's support and understanding of the child's symptoms and related behaviors (de Arellano et al., 2014). Grounded in the principles of cognitive-behavioral therapy, TF-CBT similarly emphasizes the importance of the child-caregiver relationship to help develop the child's emotional regulation and coping capabilities (de Arellano et al., 2014).

Trauma-focused cognitive behavioral therapy, like all manualized treatments, adheres to a precise therapeutic model. To ensure that the children screened to receive treatment are an appropriate fit, the therapist must possess a full comprehension of traumatic events. The core components of TF-CBT are psychoeducation about the child's identified trauma and PTSD; affective modulation skills; individualized stress-management skills; an introduction to the cognitive triad (relationships between thoughts, feelings, and behaviors); creating a trauma narrative (a gradual exposure intervention where the child describes the progressively distressing details of their trauma); cognitive processing; safety skills and education about healthy healing; and a parental treatment component (Cohen et al., 2007). The total comprehension of the primary traumatic event is provided within the child's own self-identified narrative of trauma. TF-CBT provides an intervention by which a child can address the stigmatization they experience as children of incarcerated parents and offers a clinical approach to help them heal from emotional, physical, and material consequences resulting from the traumatic loss of an incarcerated parent.

While the model works most efficiently for children who present higher rates of depressive symptoms and have a willingness to engage in the therapeutic process, children who are experiencing more significant symptoms of trauma avoidance and mistrust in authoritative figures may struggle to initially connect to their therapists. All therapists who employ an anti-racist and anti-oppressive practice and application will hold space for the importance of and validate the child's mistrust as several have witnessed or directly experienced police brutality. By offering the child space to normalize and unpack this fear, the gradual process and clinical partnership will be formed. While some clinicians may view this as causing some delays in the application of this time-specific framework, modifications to the initial phase are reflective of the therapist's anti-oppressive integration of necessary adaptation. In addition, one study found that symptom arousal and clinical withdrawal increased during the assessment period, suggesting that service initiation may increase symptom intensity, especially in cases where appropriate feelings of fear or mistrust are common and where children may have difficulty tolerating these arousal symptoms early in the therapeutic process (Konanur et al., 2015a). Clinicians must demonstrate patience and understanding when starting the model of meeting the child where they are.

TF-CBT requires parental involvement in treatment through periodic joint treatment sessions with the child and caregiver or guardian. These cooperative sessions aim to provide caregivers with skills that allow them to expand learning from psychotherapy into the child's home (Konanur et al., 2015a, b). As the family acquires a more comprehensive understanding of the child's symptomatology and experience, the goal of reducing the child's traumatic symptoms can be more readily achieved. When implementing TF-CBT, therapists are encouraged to adapt the model to fit the needs of the children and family members and to facilitate enhanced cognition and understanding of trauma in the caregiver. Also, given the stated effects of parental incarceration on the remaining caregivers, it is crucial to point out that the family treatment approach that is a component of TF-CBT provides opportunities for treatment of the strained caregiver responsible for the child.

TF-CBT applies a prescriptive approach according to a specific model of treatment. Research conducted by Cohen (2006) on treatment redirection has suggested that clinicians themselves may experience their own process of questioning the implementation of evidence-based treatments because they may perceive manualized models to be more rigid and less creative than other therapeutic approaches to treatment. Because TF-CBT is a short-term model, clinicians may also feel as though they are pressured by a time constraint that favors the completion of task-oriented client experiences and activities, as opposed to carrying out ad hoc clinical procedures. Clinicians may also experience their own avoidance when discussing trauma, which can hinder the clinical process further (Simonich et al., 2015). Therefore, ensuring that adequate culture-based supervision is provided to the clinician working with the family is central to unpacking any clinical bias or potential for harm.

Advantages of TF-CBT Applications

In 15 randomized controlled trials that evaluated TF-CBT, the treatment group experienced significantly improved symptomatology compared to the control group across outcome measures examining PTSD, depression, anxiety, behavioral, cognitive, relationship, and other problems (Cohen & Mannarino, 2015). A meta-analysis pertaining to children and adolescents (de Arellano et al., 2014) concluded that TF-CBT is associated with improved child and caregiver outcomes; individuals experiencing symptoms of post-traumatic stress performed significantly better than individuals in comparison groups. The findings for treatment of individuals with depression symptoms was less robust, however, showing that in five out of nine studies examined, TF-CBT produced a medium-sized effect compared to individuals not receiving treatment. Findings for individuals experiencing other behavioral problems, such as depressive and withdrawn behavior, were mixed. The research (de Arellano et al., 2014) suggests that the application and usage of TF-CBT is expanding and that even with wider dissemination, fidelity to the model remains strong, which may suggest some ease in the implementation of the model.

A more recent randomized controlled trial (Konanur et al., 2015a, b) found that TF-CBT significantly reduced post-traumatic stress symptomatology during the observed treatment period, suggesting that engagement in this therapeutic process drives positive outcomes. Furthermore, their research provided interesting insights into the specific processes, mechanisms, and contributions of the TF-CBT process. Konanur et al. (2015a, b) were able to hypothesize that positive outcomes related to symptom improvement during the assessment period may be related to hope or an optimistic outlook by the client during the introductory period.

The Substance Abuse and Mental Health Services Administration lists trauma-focused cognitive behavioral therapy as a therapy "with effective outcomes" for some treatment conditions and "promising" for all other conditions within its National Registry of Evidence-Based Programs and Practices (SAMHSA, 2015). In numerous studies, TF-CBT is shown to significantly reduce trauma symptomatology (de Arellano et al., 2014; Konanur et al., 2015a). In their meta-analysis, Ramirez et al. (2014) concluded that TF-CBT is effective at treating highly vulnerable populations, such as children who are at risk for violence, suicidality, psychosis, and/or substance abuse, as well as those who are developmentally disabled.

Recent research shows that children exposed to interpersonal violence and treated with TF-CBT experienced lower rates of relapse into PTSD symptomatology than the non-treatment group (Cohen et al., 2011). Children who experience parental incarceration fall within the target population to receive the TF-CBT intervention as parental incarceration is considered an adverse childhood experience with the potential to be traumatic for the child (Afifi et al., 2011; Arditti & Savla, 2015). Many children affected by parental incarceration experience depression, social and emotional distress reinforced by systemic racism and oppression, and externalizing behaviors that are symptoms of trauma.

Case Example of TF-CBT Treatment for Children Traumatized by Parental Incarceration

The following case study is an example of a local deployment of TF-CBT treatment to a child and caregiver father within a community-based outpatient setting. This case study discusses the associations between parental incarceration and the development of trauma-related symptomatology, the treatment conditions addressed through the TF-CBT intervention, initial outcomes from treatment, as well as the implications for TF-CBT utility for children affected by parental incarceration. In this description of their treatment, all names and identifying information have been altered to protect patient confidentiality. Signed informed consent for publishing this case example was obtained by the caregiver and the child assented.

Presenting Problem: Case Conceptualization

Carrie,[1] a 30-year-old woman, sought mental health services for her 9-year-old daughter, Daliah. During an initial telephone screening with a supervising clinician, Carrie explained that she was incarcerated at a New York State correctional facility and had been referred to the clinic because of its mission to work with children and families affected by incarceration. Carrie provided an initial history and background information for her family. Carrie had been physically and sexually assaulted on numerous occasions over the course of 10 years by her daughter's father, Tony. Carrie's daughter, Daliah, had witnessed fighting between her parents on numerous occasions.

On the night of the arrest that led to Carrie's incarceration, she used self-defense during a brutal physical attack that included an attempted rape and led to the death of Daliah's father. Daliah witnessed the conflict between her mother and father, was present when the paramedics arrived to remove her father, and when the police arrived to handcuff and remove her mother.

While her mother was detained, Daliah was placed in kinship care with her paternal grandmother. Carrie reported that Daliah had become emotionally withdrawn in the immediate period following her arrest and detention and began to exhibit certain trauma responses at school, which led to detention and other challenges. Carrie admitted that she was still struggling with the emotional effects of the sustained assault and victimization and had been recently diagnosed with complex PTSD.

Carrie received a conditional early release from prison and returned home as her legal team was able to provide ample evidence of the years she endured and survived inter-partner violence. She resumed care of Daliah, still under the kinship care with her paternal grandfather, and quickly decided to meet with clinicians for an in-person intake and assessment. Clinicians conducted an initial screening with both Carrie and Daliah present. The initial intake was an opportunity for clinicians to support Carrie and Daliah, discuss their feelings about the incarceration, and identify the residual traumatic clinical implications of these events. During the first session of the intake, clinicians met with the child and caregiver together. Carrie explained that she understood that Daliah had acted out in anger and rage on multiple occasions in school, which resulted in numerous suspensions. During this initial intake, Carrie revealed that she had felt "afraid" for her daughter and "ashamed" while she was incarcerated. Carrie presented herself as someone with significant anxiety, fear, and a negative sense of self, which was driven by the continual trauma and hopelessness she felt during her imprisonment. "I couldn't help her," she told the clinicians. As part of the screening process, clinicians directly engaged Daliah in a discussion around the altercation that resulted in Carrie's arrest and attempted to identify her thoughts and feelings surrounding the traumatic event and the subsequent years of her mother's imprisonment.

[1] Pseudonyms are used in this chapter to preserve confidentiality.

Application of TF-CBT with Carrie and Daliah

Over two 90-minute intake sessions, the clinical team administered a comprehensive biopsychosocial assessment, trauma assessment and checklist, PTSD-Reaction Index, adult trauma checklist, and psychiatric evaluations to identify any ongoing chronic traumatic stress and symptoms experienced by both Carrie and Daliah. A clinical treatment plan was established for both clients, which recommended that Carrie and Daliah would each be seen once weekly for individual psychotherapy. The treatment plan also recommended that the family receive joint sessions on a bi-weekly basis over the course of 18 weeks. During this intake process, the clinicians explained to the family that they would be utilizing TF-CBT with three phases of the model. The model was described in further detail to the family as consisting of the following three phases: (1) the stabilization phase; (2) the trauma narrative phase; and (3) the integration/consolidation phase. A brief description of the activities and purposes of each phase was also described during this assessment.

Phase 1: Stabilization

During the stabilization phase of the model, clinicians used psychoeducation to discuss trauma and inter-partner violence with Carrie and Daliah within sessions one to three. The clinicians determined that psychoeducation around these subjects was necessary because Daliah commonly expressed feeling as though "daddy beat up mommy because she was in trouble" instead of recognizing the specific dynamic of abuse and trauma. When describing instances of her own abuse, Carrie shared that she "just thought bad things always happened," showing evidence of dysfunctional cognitions (Unterhitzenberger & Rosner, 2016) commonly expressed in victimization and abuse.

Throughout sessions four to seven of both individual psychotherapy and joint sessions during this phase, Daliah reported that many children at school would taunt her for being parentless throughout the period of her mother's incarceration. Community members called Carrie a "monster" and "murderer" in front of Daliah, who lashed out at her mother for "taking away [her] daddy." In individual psychotherapy sessions with the caregiver during this phase, clinicians helped Carrie connect her daughter's behavioral challenges to the traumatic experiences being discussed in their therapeutic process. The clinicians aided Carrie in embracing a holistic perspective of the reason for her daughter's behavior through employing the Cognitive Triangle to accurately identify her feelings and better understand how her thoughts and feelings impacted her reactions toward her daughter. As a result, Carrie was able to regulate her reactive responses to her daughter's anger through the application of parenting exercises where she engaged in her own process on how to provide Daliah with praise and reinforcement, as well as selective attention when she would respond with anger. This allowed Daliah to have room to safely express herself without Carrie personalizing her responses.

Daliah responded strongly to the mindfulness practices and focused breathing techniques taught during sessions eight and nine of this phase. She explained that, when provoked, she would "fight anyone who got near [her]" and her grandfather revealed that she had been suspended several times during her mother's incarceration and was unable to trust any adult figures because she feared they would leave her. The clinician aided Daliah in understanding the physiology of relaxation and how she could successfully regain control over her body when she felt angry or upset. When she began to successfully implement these relaxation and mindfulness practices at school, such as deep breathing and positive self-talk, the family, and Daliah herself, expressed excitement that she was reportedly no longer responding to her classmates with anger; she stated, "I feel powerful over my own body today." The clinicians taught relaxation through guided meditation and affective regulation skills, which enabled Carrie to recount the abuse and torture she endured. She was also able to recall how she would go into fits of rage, or "blackouts," that she would not remember. Through cognitive processing, an integral element of the stabilization phase, the social workers explained to Carrie that these "blackouts" were, in fact, symptoms of trauma, a protective factor against the abuse she endured. The stabilization phase of the model also helped both participants prepare for the narrative writing that would be executed in the next phase.

Phase 2: Trauma Narrative

Completion of the first phase of the TF-CBT model facilitated Daliah's understanding of the abuse her mother suffered and that the act that led to her incarceration was carried out in self-defense. While Daliah identified her mother's incarceration as her primary traumatic loss, she also included a chapter on losing her father, which the clinician and Carrie supported, as it remained critical that she narrate her own experience. Daliah reported "missing him very much" and that he "was my daddy no matter what, even though I missed my mommy so much." When it came time for Daliah to write and deliver her trauma narrative to Carrie, she chose to focus her story on her father's loss and her mother's arrest.

In sessions 10–12, Daliah developed her first draft of the narrative. During the formulation of the narrative, Daliah developed an interest in better understanding the events surrounding the night of her father's passing and expressed a desire to ask her mother questions about the events in their joint family sessions. Daliah shared feeling "not as angry" and "just sad because I lost my mommy for two years and my daddy for good all in one night." She wanted to know if she "would ever get another daddy again." Daliah included these feelings in the narrative and had an emotional and powerful reading of the story in session 13. This was the first time her mother heard from Daliah that she did not blame Carrie for protecting herself, but that she needed to share her feelings of pain and sadness for no longer having her father.

Daliah was able to vocalize her feelings and Carrie was willing to listen without reacting in a personalized manner. Through the reading of the narrative, Daliah no longer covered her face when showing emotional avoidance, as she once did; instead, she was able to confront her fears and speak directly to her mother. Daliah said she learned to do this by deep breathing instead of hiding her face.

Phase 3: Integration/Consolidation

During sessions 14–17, the final phase of treatment, the clinicians continued joint parent-child sessions. Daliah and Carrie enhanced their overall communication and developed and practiced a safety plan to address her social and emotional behaviors (e.g., deep breathing, conflict mediation). Daliah and Carrie spoke openly about the trauma they experienced during Carrie's incarceration and the death of Daliah's father. Carrie expressed feeling "hopeful about [their] growing relationship." Because she was able to address the overwhelming shame and guilt engendered during her imprisonment, Daliah's self-esteem and self-efficacy improved dramatically throughout the course of treatment through self-reports in both individual and family therapy. The narrative sharing process facilitated the development of trust between the child and caregiver. Although she initially was afraid to express her desire for her mother's protection from the community's shame and stigmatization, the narrative process enabled Daliah to share her true feelings with her mother and "feel safe to share everything with [her]." In their last session, they reported that they had a plan to "move forward and grow as a family."

Case Discussion

This case demonstrates that TF-CBT can be effectively used with a child and parent suffering from traumatic symptoms related to parental incarceration and other complex traumas. The case illustrates how the core concepts of this model allowed for the family to speak openly and safely about the trauma without feeling afraid that any member would become overwhelmed or upset when speaking about the traumatic separation during the incarceration. This particular illustration underlines the importance of both the child and parent participating in their own therapy as well as the outlined joint sessions within the model, so that each client can share their concerns in the joint sessions without causing more distress.

The description of the phases throughout the case illustration conveys that no significant variations were made to the model by the clinicians. To maintain anti-racist and anti-oppressive practices, the clinicians and family members spread out the trauma narrative over three sessions, as Daliah expressed a desire to "take [her] time to remember everything" and had stated, "I can't trust this white lady overnight" when first meeting her clinician. The clinician addressed and named this an appropriate response to mistrust and assured Daliah she would only move at her desired pace. This practice would be used with any child throughout the course of treatment and does not delineate from the guidelines of TF-CBT (Cohen et al., 2006a, b). Using the psychoeducation offered throughout the model, Carrie was able to comprehend a more accurate depiction of her years of abuse and what essentially led to her having to defend herself that night. This allowed Carrie to feel relieved of the guilt and excessive worry she felt when Daliah would become angry at her during arguments at home, and Carrie successfully responded with patience. When the model concluded, the family revealed feeling "tighter" and "closer" than they had prior to Carrie's incarceration. Both Carrie and Daliah verbally reported feeling that their symptomatology had improved and that they had attained the goals established in their treatment plans.

The presentation of this case study should provide promising initial evidence for the successful utilization of TF-CBT treatment for children and families affected by parental incarceration. A case example provides only limited evidence for the treatment model's success, and additional research must be conducted to develop more conclusive evidence that TF-CBT is an effective treatment model for this population. The results presented through this case example should encourage future researchers to explore this treatment intervention with a larger sample to produce results that are more generalizable and conclusive. Children of incarcerated parents are not a nominal population, and additional research into TF-CBT success with this population is further justified by the need for self-driven narratives used to heal from the trauma associated with mass incarceration.

Reflection Questions

1. In your clinical opinion, is modification of length to TF-CBT therapeutically flexible depending on the client's trauma?
2. Describe the specific phases of TF-CBT and identify which phase you feel would be the most impactful for you as the clinician.
3. How have you dealt with avoidance in clients when utilizing an evidence-based practice that has a specific number of sessions required?
4. What were your personal reactions to Daliah's decision to focus on her mom's arrest as her primary trauma?

References

Afifi, T., Mather, A., Boman, J., Fleisher, W., Enns, M., MacMillan, H., & Sareen, J. (2011). Childhood adversity and personality disorders: Results from a nationally representative population-based study. *Journal of Psychiatric Research*, *45*, 814–822.

Arditti, J., & Savla, J. (2015). Parental incarceration and child trauma symptoms in single caregiver homes. *Journal of Child and Family Studies*, *24*(3), 551–561.

Cohen, J. (2006). Social, emotional, ethical, and academic education: Creating a climate for learning, participation in democracy, and well-being. *Harvard educational review*, *76*(2), 201–237.

Cohen, J. A,, Mannarino, A. P., Perel, J. M., & Staron, V. (2007). A pilot randomized controlled trial of combined trauma-focused CBT and sertraline for childhood PTSD symptoms. *Journal of the American Academy of Child & Adolescent Psychiatry, 46*(7):811–819.

Cohen, J., & Mannarino, A. (2015). Trauma-focused cognitive behavior therapy for traumatized children and families. *Child and Adolescent Psychiatric Clinics of North America, 24*, 557–570.

Cohen, J., Mannarino, A., & Deblinger, E. (2006a). Trauma focused cognitive behavioral therapy for sexually abused children. *Psychiatric Times, XXII*(10).

Cohen, J., Mannarino, A., & Deblinger, E. (2006b). *Treating trauma and traumatic grief in children and adolescents.* New York: Guilford, p.1–345.

Cohen, J., Mannarino, A., & Iyengar, S. (2011). Community treatment of posttraumatic stress disorder for children exposed to intimate partner violence: A randomized controlled trial. *Archives of Pediatric Adolescent Medicine, 165*(1), 16–21.

de Arellano, M. A. R., Lyman, D. R., Jobe-Shields, L., George, P., Dougherty, R. H., Daniels, A. S., …, Delphin-Rittmon, M. E. (2014). Trauma-focused cognitive-behavioral therapy for children and adolescents: Assessing the evidence. *Psychiatric Services, 65*(5), 591–602.

Erickson, A. L., Engel, K., Hoesel, J., Wonderlich, S. A., Myers, T. C., Simonich, H. K., & Wagner, S. (2015). A statewide trauma-focused cognitive behavioral therapy network: Creating an integrated community response. *Journal of Contemporary Psychotherapy, 45*, 265–274.

Konanur, S., Muller, R. T., Cinamon, J. S., Thornback, K., & Zorella, K. (2015a). Effectiveness of trauma-focused cognitive behavioral therapy in a community-based program. *Child Abuse and Neglect: The International Journal, 50*, 259–170.

Konanur, S., Muller, R. T., Cinamon, J. S., Thornback, K., & Zorella, K. (2015b). Effectiveness of trauma-focused cognitive behavioral therapy in a community-based program. *Child Abuse and Neglect The International Journal, 50: 259–170.*

Manning, R. (2011). Punishing the innocent: Children of incarcerated and detained parents. *Criminal Justice Ethics, 30*(3), 267–287.

Miller, H. V., & Barnes, J. C. (2015). The association between parental incarceration and health, education, and economic outcomes in young adulthood. *American Journal of Criminal Justice, 40*, 765–784.

Murray, J., Farrington, D. P., & Sekol, I. (2012). Children's antisocial behavior, mental health, drug use, and educational performance after parental incarceration: A systematic review and meta-analysis. *Psychological Bulletin, 138*(2), 175–210.

Phillips, S. D., Erkanki, A., Keeler, G. P., Costello, E. J., & Angold, A. (2006). Disentangling the risks: Parents criminal justice involvement and children's exposure to family risks. *Criminology & Public Policy, 5*(4), 677–702.

Ramirez, M. A., Lyman, R. D., George, P., Shields, J. L., Dougherty, R. H., Daniels, A. S., Ghose, S. S., Huang, L., & Delphin-Rittmon, M. E. (2014). Trauma-focused cognitive-behavioral therapy for children and adolescents: Assessing the evidence. *Psychiatric Services, 65*(5), 591–602.

Simonich, H. K., Wonderlich, S. A., Erickson, A. L., Myers, T. C., Hoesel, J., Wagner, S., & Engel, K. (2015). A statewide trauma-focused cognitive behavioral therapy network: Creating an integrated community response system. *Journal of Contemporary Psychotherapy, 45*(4), 265–274.

Substance Abuse and Mental Health Services Administration (SAMHSA). (2015). *Evidence-based practices resource center*. Accessible at: https://www.samhsa.gov/resource-search/ebp

Unterhitzenberger, J., & Rosner, R. (2016). Case report: Manualized trauma-focused cognitive behavioral therapy with an unaccompanied refugee minor girl. *European Journal of Pychotraumatology, 7*, 1–5.

Chapter 6
Prolonged Exposure Therapy for PTSD

Addressing Trauma Symptoms with Prolonged Explore Therapy

A necessary intervention to working with children impacted by parental incarceration must include the reunification of family systems when a parent returns home. Many parents return home with extensive trauma as they have survived a brutalizing system of violence which can increase feelings of fear, anxiety, mistrust, and anger, which clinicians will include in the family work required for successful reunification and re-stabilization. Prolonged Exposure Therapy (PE) addresses trauma at the source and facilitates emotional processing by decreasing feelings of numbness where individuals are then able to regain access to their feelings and confront cognitive responses instead of reactions rooted in fear. It assesses the full trauma history which will include the parent's trauma prior to incarceration, during incarceration, and the anxiety of integrating back into familial and community-based settings.

Prolonged Exposure Therapy for PTSD offers psychoeducation on trauma, education about common reactions to trauma, rationale for how PE can help decrease PTSD, breathing training, imaginal exposure to trauma memory (revisiting and recounting), and repeated in vivo exposure to safe situations that are avoided because of trauma-related fear (Foa et al., 2007). Treatment consists of an average of 10 to 12 90-minute sessions. This course of treatment is commonly used when disconfirming that anxiety and fear will last forever. The application of this particular therapeutic intervention works to unpack the misconceptions that once an individual returns from a carceral setting, they will permanently struggle to undo the trauma they endured in that oppressive space. Clinicians working with children and their family members who have experienced grief and traumatic loss due to these systems can employ this practice as a hopeful and healing component to reconnecting family when the child's loved one returns home. The case illustration below

A. Morgan-Mullane, *An Integrative Approach to Clinical Social Work Practice with Children of Incarcerated Parents*, Essential Clinical Social Work Series,
https://doi.org/10.1007/978-3-031-28823-4_6

highlights this successful clinical intervention as a formative tool in addressing traumatic stress in both the parents and their children when they return from prison or jail.

Case Illustration

Trayvon came to Children of Promise, NYC Wellness Center for therapeutic services after his girlfriend, who is seeking treatment at our clinic, requested that he come. She shared during her family session that he had been suffering from multiple panic attacks and was struggling to function outside of the house. Trayvon was initially appropriately apprehensive to treatment but after his most recent panic attack outside with the family while at the beach, he agreed to be seen for an intake.

During the initial assessment with intake, Trayvon disclosed he had been incarcerated for most of his life. Now, at 33 years old, he was out of prison and trying to "live a normal life with [his] girlfriend and her children." Trayvon shared that he has longed for family and normalcy as he has been in and out of state prisons since the age of 13. He disclosed that his incarceration was mostly gang related and having accepted bids for other gang members instead of "selling out his brothers." Trayvon became tearful throughout the intake when disclosing the pain and suffering he endured in prison. He witnessed events such as murders between inmates, murders between correctional officers and inmates, he himself had been physically and sexually abused by inmates as well as officers, and he currently experiences flashbacks, nightmares, and a fear of crowds.

Assessment

The clinician conducting the intake obtained a detailed trauma history of the incarcerations, violence, and abuse he suffered, and Trayvon could identify that the index trauma (Foa et al., 2007) was the incident where he was rushed in his cell by the correctional officers, 10 of them, and was beaten until both arms, four ribs, and his leg were broken. He stated that this particular incident has caused tremendous fear when he is out in crowds as he feels overwhelmed, scared, anxious, and fearful and has flashbacks of being in his small cell and having 10 people violently beat him up. Because he presently exhibited severe symptoms of PTSD and other related psychopathology such as chronic anxiety and high levels of anger (Foa et al., 2007), the clinician conducting the intake confirmed that Trayvon met the criteria for PTSD and felt Prolonged Exposure Therapy (PE) would be the most appropriate treatment model for him to participate in as he also conveyed a sufficient memory of the traumatic events which allowed for him to have a clear narrative (Foa et al., 2007) to complete the model.

Starting Treatment

Session 1

At the start of the first session, the clinician gave Trayvon a rationale for PE and discussed the main tools of the model, which include imaginal and in vivo exposure (Foa et al., 2007). Because Trayvon had repeatedly stated throughout the intake process that he felt "something was wrong" with him and that he feared he was "crazy," the clinician assured him this particular therapeutic approach aids the client in learning that they can in fact tolerate their distress and the anxiety he may experience does not mean he is going to lose control or go crazy (McLean & Foa, 2013). This allowed for Trayvon to feel more comfortable as he regularly felt he was "crazy" and that being in any environment that would cause him to feel anxious would confirm that he was. After the overview of treatment was explained, the therapist provided psychoeducation about his symptoms as described above, and this again offered Trayvon the opportunity to continually acknowledge that what he had been secretly holding in for fear of being told he was "insane" was in fact normal PTSD symptoms. He expressed relief in learning about what trauma was and what his symptoms were as they related to his index trauma. The clinician then introduced breathing retraining at the end of the first session, which would become his tool to practice at home for his homework for the week. The session concluded with Trayvon being instructed to practice this type of breathing for 10 minutes, twice a day. The session had been audiotaped so he could listen to their session at home in privacy prior to the next session and he would also complete the Rationale for Treatment workbook, which would be reviewed in the following session. Trayvon expressed his excitement of overcoming his anxiety and conveyed a strong willingness to engage in treatment.

Session 2

The second session began with an overview of his homework. Trayvon expressed his ability to try out the breathing techniques, but he struggled to complete the workbook. The clinician and Trayvon explored the reasons behind this, and he expressed his own anxiety about reading and writing as he had difficulty comprehending the information in the workbook. They agreed to review it together and go through the homework more carefully in follow-up sessions to assure that he understood that material and not assume that the homework would come easily to him. The clinician continued with the session by continuing to educate Trayvon about his PTSD symptoms and normalized his anxiety and fear by highlighting how much anxiety is a natural response (Back et al., 2014) to trauma and how fearful he may feel when he is in crowded situations, which remind him of the previous dangerous situations he was in when he was incarcerated.

The second part of the session included the clinician providing examples of in vivo exposures to help Trayvon understand how the process works as well as to demystify the process. The clinician then offered an introduction to the Subjective Units of Distress Scale (SUDS) prior to constructing a hierarchy of feared and avoided situations. Trayvon engaged in this scale and confirmed his own interpretation of the numbers used when the clinician confirmed she would be using them throughout the remaining sessions when she would check in with him. Trayvon and the clinician then constructed his in vivo exposure hierarchy. This was simple for Trayvon to complete as he could easily identify certain behaviors of his in terms of avoidance. He disclosed that the situations he perceives that are dangerous that he avoids includes "any types of crowds, so going on the bus, restaurants with [his] family, and the beach." He feels strongly that if he is to go to these particular places, he is putting himself and his family at risk. The second situations he disclosed were those that remind him of the event such as seeing blood if one of his daughters cuts herself on accident, watching any movies that have police officers, or walking on certain blocks in his neighborhood where there are a lot of "cop cars." The clinician and Trayvon closed the session by identifying the safety consideration when completing his hierarchy and he acknowledged that there are certain blocks that are "too triggering right now" for him to walk down that he would like to avoid for his personal safety.

After the completion of his In Vivo Exposure Hierarchy, as shown below, the clinician and Trayvon decided together which situations he would confront for his homework. They started with the situations that were rated between 40 and 50 on his SUDS and then reviewed how he would complete the homework after the exposure is complete. Trayvon confirmed that he wanted to try going to dinner with his girlfriend and the beach with his daughters for his in vivo exposure homework based.

Item	SUDS Session 2	SUDS Session 9	SUDS Final Session
Going out to eat with my girlfriend	50		
Going out to eat as a family	60		
Going to the beach in the summer	75		
Going down the block my brothers live on	90		
Going to a club	95		
Going to the grocery store	65		
Going to gatherings for family members	65		

Session 3

In session 3, Trayvon and the clinician reviewed his homework, where he could share what he had learned from doing the exposure. Trayvon reported feeling as though the homework was very helpful, and he only had one panic attack that "didn't last that long" during dinner with his girlfriend. He stated he had to leave the lounge "only once" later in the evening as the "crowds became too much" but that he could "successfully go to the beach" with his daughters, who praised him the entire time, making him feel proud. Trayvon was then asked to access his traumatic events by sharing thoughts, emotions, and sensory experiences. The client continued to discuss the memory of having been viciously assaulted in his prison cell by the 10 officers, as it had been the primary memory that was causing the most distressing thoughts, flashbacks, and nightmares. He was asked to process this trauma for 15–20 minutes in which he would talk about his reactions to revisiting the trauma (Foa et al., 2007) by imaginal recounting of the memory. Throughout the imaginal exposure, the clinician offered supportive language when it was clear he was becoming distressed, such as "you're doing so well, keep going" and "I know this is difficult, but you are doing such an excellent job" as well as "you're safe here, you can keep going." After the 20 minutes concluded, the clinician supported Trayvon in discussing his experience where he could report that it "did not feel as bad as [he] thought it would." Trayvon was instructed to listen to the recording at home in between sessions and record his SUDS level. He was then instructed to choose another in vivo exposure, which he stated would be going to a family event with his girlfriend and attempting to go to the grocery store as well.

Intermediate Sessions: 4–9

Throughout sessions 4 through 9, the clinician and Trayvon continued to review his homework from each week and work through his imaginal exposure. The clinician introduced the concept of "hot spots," in which the client gives the highest SUDS score during this imaginal exposure. The clinician reviewed the definition of habituation and how Trayvon's ability to move through this hot spot in his narrative would allow him to move through the feelings of fear and anxiety more smoothly and practice his in vivo exposures more easily. Trayvon acknowledged that he most commonly becomes anxious when describing the part in his trauma where he could "feel [his] arm being broken and watching the blood from [his] head pool up around [him] on the floor." Trayvon reported this is where he becomes the most "fearful and angry" and wants to "avoid thinking about it altogether." However, in identifying this hot spot and working throughout the sessions to discuss it more comfortably, he reported at the end of the ninth session that his SUDS score went from a 90 to a 40, for which the clinician praised him extensively. To conclude these sessions, Trayvon was asked to listen to the imaginal exposure tape daily and continue to practice his in vivo exposure exercises.

Final Session

The final session began with reviewing the homework and the SUDS ratings. Trayvon was then asked to recount the entire trauma memory rather than working on the hot spots they had addressed in previous sessions. The clinician praised Trayvon throughout and then concluded the session by reviewing their progress in the treatment model and explored the In Vivo Exposure Hierarchy created in the second session. Trayvon reported feeling as though he accomplished his changes, and his family expressed their pride in his ability to now go out to eat, go to the store, and go to the beach together without him having a panic attack. The clinician praised the client for the extensive drop in his SUDS ratings and how supported he felt by his family and therapist in working through a fear he never imagined he would be able to "get over."

Item	SUDS Session 2	SUDS Session 9	SUDS Final Session
Going out to eat with my girlfriend	50	20	0
Going out to eat as a family	60	15	0
Going to the beach in the summer	75	30	10
Going down the block my brothers live on	90	80	70
Going to a club	95	60	20
Going to the grocery store	65	40	20
Going to gatherings for family members	65	35	10

Trayvon expressed gratitude for overcoming his fear, an outcome he felt was a direct result of this practice. He shared that he had been highly motivated but anxious about the homework and having to listen to the sessions week to week. He reported feeling "more in control" and that learning "more about [his] problems and feelings" allowed for him to begin to heal from the "darkness that time brought to [his] life and to [his] family."

Conclusion

Trayvon's experience with Prolonged Exposure Therapy signifies the importance of identifying an index trauma that has deeply impacted a client to the point of feeling paralyzed. Trayvon had not realized that after close to 20 years of incarceration, there was one specific event that he could recognize as causing the most distress in his emotional well-being, keeping him from feeling confident to participate with his family and out in the community. This was impacting his relationships with his children, his girlfriend, and ultimately his own self-esteem of not feeling as though he could control his emotions, fears, and anxiety. Trayvon took a risk in completing this model because he felt as though his anger, rage, and anxiety would debilitate him throughout the process, only to find that moving through these fears could end up healing the most torturous memory he had been carrying around for the last 2 years since he was released.

The clinician feels strongly that Trayvon should continue with ongoing supportive psychodynamic therapy to continue to process the chronic history of trauma he has that began prior to his teenage years of incarceration and continue to work on strengthening his communication with his family now that he feels more empowered in understanding his trauma symptoms.

Reflection Questions

1. How would you employ the SUDS scale with a client who presents with complex trauma and might struggle to specify their trauma symptoms?
2. What barriers do you feel would impact the client's ability to participate in this form of therapy when addressing index trauma?
3. How do you feel this model would best benefit your practice?

References

Back, S., Foa, E., Killeen, T., Mills, K., Teeson, M., Cotton, B., Carroll, K., & Brady, K. (2014). *Concurrent treatment of PTSD and substance use disorders using prolonged exposure (COPE): Patient workbook.* Oxford University Press.

Foa, E., Hembree, E., & Rothbaum, B. O. (2007). *Prolonged exposure therapy for PTSD: Emotional processing of traumatic experiences – Therapist guide (treatments that work).* Oxford University Press.

McLean C. P., & Foa, E. B. (2013). Dissemination and implementation of prolonged exposure therapy for posttraumatic stress disorder. *Journal of Anxiety Disorders*, *27*(8), 788–92.

Chapter 7
Attachment Theory and Relational Therapy

The effects of parental incarceration on a child are clinically similar to the experiences of children who have lost parents to divorce, death, or military deployment (Turney, 2014). John Bowlby described the deprivation of the caregiver-child relationship as significantly contributing to trauma symptoms that children internalize and have difficulty addressing without proper intervention. Attachment-based therapies and relational theory work to promote changes in an individual's feeling and thinking, with an increased sense of security. The specific clinical practices rooted in attachment and relational therapy for children of incarcerated parents emphasize the use of attachment and relational theory to undo cognitive distortions and beliefs that are common to children of incarcerated parents (e.g., others are not caring or responsive). The utilization of this overarching theory supports the child's ability to trust adults and gain a greater sense of safety in the world around them. In instances where a child loses a parent to incarceration, the clinician works in partnership with the child's attachment-based system when the threat of separation is experienced, which directly impacts their self-esteem, self-confidence, and trust in relationships.

Application of Relational-Cultural Theory in Treatment for Children of Incarcerated Parents

Constant and recurrent traumatic events that impact interpersonal security can lead to long-standing social and emotional consequences, which affect various areas of an individual's health and well-being across their life span (DiLillo, 2001; Ogle et al., 2013). Additionally, it is often understood that people who experience interpersonal traumas experience a sense of betrayal, powerlessness, and stigmatization (Deitz et al., 2015; Platt & Freyd, 2015). When these traumatic responses to feelings

A. Morgan-Mullane, *An Integrative Approach to Clinical Social Work Practice with Children of Incarcerated Parents*, Essential Clinical Social Work Series,
https://doi.org/10.1007/978-3-031-28823-4_7

of powerlessness impact children, it is likely to contribute to a distorted self-concept and worldview (Walsh et al., 2010).

Relational-Cultural Theory (RCT) employs a practice that allows for individuals to focus on connection with others throughout their life span so that, by forming and maintaining healthy relationships, they can build a sense of personal safety and well-being (Jordan, 2010). Moreover, RCT suggests that connecting with others and forming growth-fostering relationships serve as a healing mechanism (Jordan, 2010). An RCT application can provide a framework and lens from which clinicians can partner with children on how to best recognize, form, and maintain healthy relationships (Kress et al., 2018) during a time that can feel unsettling and ambiguous. Therefore, the use of RCT with children of incarcerated parents during their loss of a loved one to the carceral system is an approach that can be especially useful when naming the systems of oppression that have directly impacted the child's and parent's beliefs of safety and security in the world at large. Mental health providers working with individuals who have experienced trauma that is rooted in interpersonal victimization must consider all systems that traumatize the individual, family, and community, as well as employ an anti-racist framework of safety within the therapeutic relationship that directly names those systems when addressing intergenerational systemic trauma. The emphasis RCT places on connection with the individual and others may help to diminish trauma symptoms and facilitate healthy functioning (Kress et al., 2018).

Clinicians working directly with children impacted by parental loss due to incarceration must include the child's and parent's narratives to determine which systems have continually caused harm in the child's life. Many children within the community organization Children of Promise, NYC have shared their experiences with legal systems and how necessary it is that their therapists must hold knowledge of the history of mass incarceration. Diondre,[1] age 21, recounted how he was initially hesitant to work with a white clinician when he first sought individual psychotherapy after his mother was arrested and remained in the Rikers Island jail system waiting for her trial because she was unable to afford bail. Diondre explained, "I wasn't sure a white person would honestly understand the societal problem where they are the oppressors. I'm proud to learn about my Black culture and legacy of resistance and liberation, which carried me through the depression of my mom's trial." Diondre added that his lived experience was what allowed him to recognize his own desire for mental health counseling and how he did not want to keep his feelings of fear and anger inside. Diondre shared about meeting his therapist, Mr. Matt:

> While I was hoping to meet with a Black man, the agency told me and my dad that while they were hiring more therapists, one of their senior social workers was Mr. Matt, and Mr. Matt and I met and he told me he understood it would take a while for me to trust our relationship, if ever. He then talked about his own information on mass incarceration, slavery, and how mental health now can even be a continued practice of surveillance and monitoring if the person isn't given the room to heal how they want to. Mr. Matt told me what he

[1] Pseudonyms are used in this chapter to preserve confidentiality.

> symbolically and realistically represented with his white body and the harm that can bring to the space. He asked me to call him out on anything that happened between us that I didn't feel good about and wanted the space to feel like nothing was off-limits in our relationship. I wanted to share my experiences and I was willing to give him a try since I'd never heard a white therapist talk about slavery, mass incarceration, violent oppressive systems in mental health care, and his own role in a white saviorism profession, which he was actively dismantling. That was four years ago and he's still my therapist today. I probably started to open up around our second year working together.

Haskins and Appling (2015) wrote that "RCT suggests that traditional theories of human development and psychodynamics mistakenly and harmfully perpetuate the oppressive cycle of inaccurately pathologizing clients by disregarding the historical and systemic injustices experienced by marginalized groups" (p. 88). When interviewed, Mr. Matt shared that he specifically chose RCT as his primary therapeutic practice as the model reflects and honors Diondre's lived experiences, as well as the present and past realities of racialized violence he has experienced from oppressive systems. Mr. Matt explained:

> It was central to the building of our relationship that I not only share how I centered his experience to be the only experience in the therapeutic space, but that my physical presence as a white-bodied cis male could cause tremendous concern as his mother was abused by the police. Diondre and I would speak about racist policies that lead to mass incarceration and the present legal injustice system that remains paralleled to slavery through the current prison industrial complex. We spoke about race regularly and it was imperative that he express his feelings regarding whiteness within our relationship and how sometimes I would get it wrong and remove my white fragility or white lens that could hinder co-creating a healing space for him. If this goes unchecked by white therapists, they can recreate the harm in the therapeutic space through practices that are oppressive and harmful which was something we also talked about openly in our work.

RCT facilitates and addresses social justice within the therapeutic alliance and decreases emotional and physical separation by increasing relational connections (Jordan, 2010). Mr. Matt's work through legal advocacy with Diondre for his mother during her trial allowed Diondre to see their partnership as beyond therapeutic and one that centered on addressing the entire system of mass incarceration. This applies to the model's framework of addressing social justice and increasing Diondre and Mr. Matt's relational connections. RCT emphasizes the role of power dynamics on well-being and the role these dynamics have on perpetuating shame and feelings of unworthiness (Jordan, 2010).

In the therapeutic relationship described by Diondre, his clinician demonstrated his own relationship to the clearly oppressive systems he benefited from during the initial engagement and intake experience. This gave Diondre the opportunity to identify that he continued to feel appropriately guarded about without feeling pressure to form a relationship that did not feel comfortable to him as treatment began. Throughout their work together, Mr. Matt's training and personal commitment to anti-racism and the shared personal values informed by RCT within the therapeutic relationship structured their sessions to jointly explore Diondre's personal and familial experiences within the injustice system. Through this processing and naming, Diondre was able to communicate the rage he felt toward his mother's legal barriers. Mr. Matt's continual validation and affirming of Diondre and his family's lived experience then led to opportunities for legal advocacy that raised the therapeutic relationship to a level outside of the session. Diondre described it as "really meaningful to have a therapist get out of the office and meet me in my life spaces. Mr. Matt would go to court hearings, write letters on behalf of my mother, and speak to my mom regularly. He really understood this kind of therapy was a lot more than just talking in session."

The first practice of RCT specifies that individuals move toward growth through a relational process and toward relationships that feel supportive and safe during the course of their lives (Haskins & Appling, 2015). This incorporates the notion that relational aspects of the life span are an inescapable and an essential part of life. Therefore, the work that Diondre and Mr. Matt did within their engagement sessions included the normalizing and right-sizing of Diondre's anger about losing his mother, the stressors he experienced navigating his friendships, and the feedback people shared during her time away. Mr. Matt and Diondre focused on his personal goals of navigating relationships with boundaries while underscoring how central his relationships are to his own healing process.

The second practice, mature functioning, is characterized as movement toward mutual empathy, rather than separation (Haskins & Appling, 2015). In this process, the focus of the work is to allow for the individuals to see the impact they have on others through the here-and-now process, as well as to make space to unpack how others affect them. This permits transition in relationship—honest reflection about the negative and harmful or helpful and trusting aspects of the relationship that may require change. When Diondre would discuss his relationship with his mother in session, he would share about her strengths and the way she made him feel seen. Diondre would commonly speak about the impact this had on his relationships with friends who he felt supported him during her incarceration and the friends he felt "abandoned by" after her arrest. Mr. Matt would assist in reframing his processing of relationships and identify where Diondre felt the most safe when unpacking his loss. He described meaningful relationships with two cousins who "let [him] say whatever [he] needed to say without any judgment." He then spoke about a former girlfriend whom he broke up with during his therapeutic process because he recognized she was "speaking badly about why [his mother] did not make [him] feel safe." Navigating how he wanted to show up in each relationship was central to Diondre feeling as though he had the support group he needed to help him grow.

The third underlying principle of RCT is that relationship differentiation and elaboration illustrate growth and expansion (Haskins & Appling, 2015). This concept is described as an individual's openness and availability to investigate various relational images. This can include such examples as past relational experiences that now shape an individual's beliefs and expectations regarding current relationships. The person is then able to differentiate between negative relational images and discern helpful and positive relational images. Examples of this can include relationships that are healthy, are engaging, or create a different expectation that the individual expresses brings them more satisfaction. Throughout his sessions, Diondre and Mr. Matt would explore the specific relationships that he would describe as being "helpful," which included specific teachers, mentors, and his brothers. Diondre would then share about the people within his community that he knew were "gossiping" about his mother and that while they "may have been close once, after she went away, how they began to move was clear that [he] did not want to spend as much time with them anymore."

Diondre and Mr. Matt would center relationships that also seemed impacted by mistrust after his mother was arrested and the effect the arrest had on his belief in any adult system. Diondre was 16 when his mother was first arrested, and he would regularly share about how that trauma of losing her led to his feeling overwhelmed and angry that adults could not be trusted. In many of the sessions, Mr. Matt would normalize how Diondre felt distrust toward the adults in his life and co-create a space where Diondre would express rage by feeling "let down" by the "systems that are supposed to protect us, but actually hurt us." Diondre further explained how his school system mimicked the carceral system by punishing children for expressing emotions and criminalizing anger, which only led to further punishment. He also disclosed an example of his rage and how the school counselor wanted to "call 911 because I talked about being so angry, I wanted to kill the cops who took my mom." Diondre proceeded to share, "Whenever an adult says you can tell me the truth and nothing will happen, but when I did, I was threatened with more police, why can't they see that as more traumatizing and makes us teens want to hold everything in because nowhere is safe?" Mr. Matt fully affirmed Diondre's experience with adults as distrusting that he was met with more punishment rather than opportunities to heal.

The fourth concept is that of mutual empathy and mutual empowerment. This concept highlights that mutual empathy and empowerment are at the base of growth-fostering relationships (Haskins & Appling, 2015). Through the exploration and identification of relational interactions through a lens of empowerment, the individual with the support of the clinician can self-define how they would like to foster emotional and relational growth. Throughout Diondre and Mr. Matt's sessions, Diondre would often talk about the relationships that brought him significant meaning, such as how he saw his parents as leaders. Diondre would share that many people blamed his parents for the structural and societal-racialized violence that his mother endured being a Black woman and how he saw her as "strong and brave to live every day in America as a Black woman." Mr. Matt supported Diondre's image and belief about his mother by further exploring other Black women in his life who were also reflective of this power he witnessed in his mother that he felt gave him his own power. Diondre was able to name family members, a teacher, and his older sister as carrying the same source of strength, power, and hope. Through these examples, Diondre expressed feeling hopeful in his community and family that he could continue to look to these women for strength the way he had with his mother.

Another primary concept of RCT is that mutual empathy and mutual empowerment are at the core of growth-fostering relationships (Haskins & Appling, 2015). With Diondre and Mr. Matt's work on exploring and identifying relational interactions that are more empowering for Diondre, such as his relationship with his mother, father, community members, and now professors in college, Diondre reported he was able to foster emotional and relational growth within the last 2 years of their therapeutic work together. RCT specifies that authenticity is necessary for real engagement and that the individual must feel as if they can be wholly themselves without judgment or critique (Haskins & Appling, 2015). Diondre expressed how he eventually felt as though he could be "unfiltered" and that it was "really a space I made my own." Through this process, Diondre explained that Mr. Matt contributed to normalizing everything he felt through a lens of combating the injustice Diondre directly experienced. This then permitted Diondre to feel his own inner power and believe that it was a healing space without judgment or criticism by his therapist or himself. This gave him greater perspective on detaching from his anger in a healthy capacity and permitted him to look to the solution he felt brought the greatest amount of release from the barriers he experienced within the broader society.

Application of Attachment Theory in Treatment for Children of Incarcerated Parents

Attachment theory (Bowlby, 1973) demonstrated the intensity of forced separation between a child and primary caregiver that can disrupt their emotional, psychological, and relational bonds, harming the child's social and emotional well-being (Solomon & Zweig, 2006; Sroufe, 1988). This forced separation, a result of parental incarceration, is even more detrimental than divorce and other forms of parent-child separation (Geller et al., 2009) as the level of ambiguous loss manifesting in fear and anxiety is significantly higher with incarceration and the trauma of parental arrest. The attachment theory literature highlights the importance of emotionally open communication in relationships. Telling children about difficult situations in honest, sensitive, and developmentally appropriate ways affirms their trust in caregivers. In contrast, when information is hidden, is distorted in a manner that contradicts the child's experience, or includes details that frighten a child, distrust or mental health problems may ensue (Bowlby, 1973). Applications of attachment theory also provide an intervention by which a child can address the stigmatization they experience as children of incarcerated parents and offer a clinical approach to help them heal from emotional, physical, and material consequences resulting from the traumatic loss of an incarcerated parent.

Parents who are incarcerated report that, prior to incarceration, they were greatly involved with daily activities that could include household chores, playing games with their children, and morning and bedtime routines (Waller & Swisher, 2006). In contrast, fewer than one-third of parents in prison, mainly fathers, see their children on a consistent basis (Hairston, 1998). This causes substantial disruption of attachment to the child's social, physical, psychological, and emotional relationship to self and others, on a daily basis. When the parent is incarcerated in a facility several hours away from their community and family, transportation to these facilities can be extremely challenging for families to attain (Arditti et al., 2003; Comfort, 2008). These physical and structural barriers limit physical connection between incarcerated parents and their children (Arditti & Savla, 2005; Edin et al., 2004; Roy & Dyson, 2005). Consequently, children's interactions with their incarcerated parents are restricted in both quantity and quality, which then results in emotional and psychological destructive consequences for their full self-development (Waller & Swisher, 2006).

Sonkin (2005) proposed that attachment style can be changed throughout a therapeutic relationship. He suggested further that adult attachment style research demonstrates that there is continuity in an individual's childhood throughout their adolescence and into adulthood in the way the individual responds to their anxiety and how they manage their own responses to feelings while lacking positive physical or emotional attachment experience with the primary caretaker early in life (Blakely & Dziadosz, 2015). Sonkin explained that a clinician can become a secure clinical base and reinforce the possibility of strengthening one's sense of self from the trusting relationship shared by the client and clinician. Therefore, the adult position of attachment figure within the clinician's symbolic role can support the healing and undoing that a client can experience and work toward achieving a secure attachment style that is characteristic of a positive sense of self, as well as growth in their beneficial understanding of their overall mental health (Blakely & Dziadosz, 2015).

When working with children of incarcerated parents, clinicians must consider the importance of entering into the relationship with that child by building a secure attachment style. A clinician must take into account how their primary role is to establish a secure clinical space and relationship with the child, which will then provide the opportunity for positive exploration by the client regarding their primary attachment figure. The clinician will ensure that while using attachment-based therapy, the assessment phase allows for the child to discuss their own relationship to their incarcerated parent as well as their other parent or caretaker who actively cares for them at home. The child's ability to share their own description of the adults in their life and have the clinician support these descriptions then generates confidence in the child's ability to be comfortable in maintaining attachment relationships, even when those figures are not readily available (Blakely & Dziadosz, 2015). The clinician affirming and validating the child's lived experiences of their parents also stimulates a feeling of being cared for by others (Blakely & Dziadosz, 2015). Insecure attachment styles are characterized by negative working models in which an individual has diminished self-esteem and low self-confidence. This contributes to a lack of trust in interpersonal relationships with others and is compounded by the observations of others who are not caring and responsive (Mikulincer & Shaver, 2007). Children of incarcerated parents have experienced several intrusive and distrustful interactions with authoritative figures, which all impact the loss of their primary caretaker to the carceral system. Therefore, this therapeutic model and practice of healing their attachment to adult figures in their life and surrounding community can be central to a healing process of forming a stronger sense of self and connection to those around them. By further unpacking the feelings of violent disruption to their ability to have a meaningful routine with their parent due to structural barriers limiting their physical contact with their parent, the clinician can aid in the positive memories and beliefs about that parent to assist in the process of healing the child's distrust.

Clinical Employment of Attachment-Based Practice with Children of Incarcerated Parents

Clinicians can expansively use attachment theory for the assessment and treatment of the psychosocial barriers children of incarcerated parents are presented with. Clinicians are trained to be thoughtful and creative in developing an individual's social histories and are experienced in obtaining the information that can be interpreted in the context of attachment theory (Blakely & Dziadosz, 2015). After the assessment phase, clinicians should then plan innovative intervention strategies to assist children in organizing authentic and unique pathways to adjust and empower change toward positive self-talk and dismantle a negative sense of self and strengthen object-working models. These necessary adjustments move the individual toward the objective of adopting a secure attachment style. When the child is provided with the opportunity to share about the impact of that loss with their incarcerated parent, there is an opening to address any inaccurate perceptions of self. For example, Trevor, who is 6 years old, believed his father's arrest was due to his behavior in school. The therapist used their trusting relationship to support the beginning phases of Trevor reshaping his relationship with his father and address the cognitive distortions that his father's arrest was connected to his disciplinary experience at school. Trevor shared:

> My big brother picked me up from school and told me daddy was in jail. I was scared to tell my mommy that I was in trouble for fighting and I thought my daddy was arrested because I got in trouble for fighting. In therapy with my mommy, Ms. Grace told me it wasn't my fault and my mommy said it wasn't my fault. Ms. Grace helped me, and I'm still mad at the police for taking my daddy, but I know it wasn't my fault and it isn't my teacher Ms. Debbie's fault.

Within their relationship with Ms. Grace, Trevor and his mother had been able to securely attach themselves to the clinician, who worked especially hard to build a trusting and consistent relationship with the family after Trevor's father was arrested. Within the consistency of their sessions, Trevor was able to do the therapeutic work of recalling painful dysfunctional and maladaptive beliefs about distrust of adults in his life after his father's arrest. Once he was able to access examples of these beliefs that were harming his ability to connect to others, then the behaviors, memories, and emotions that had contributed to an insecure adaptive style and the accompanying inefficient working models transitioned in a way that allowed Trevor to begin to positively attach to his clinician, his school counselor, and his teacher.

Attachment-based therapies with children of incarcerated parents also offer space to examine current relationships to identify thinking and behaviors characteristic of an insecure attachment style. When Trevor and Ms. Grace explored these relationships through attachment play-based therapies, Trevor began to reflect on his maladaptive responses in these relationships and relate them to events and experiences that supported the establishment of new attachment styles and working models of attachment. Examples included Trevor's ability to recognize how he displayed appropriate feelings of anger and loss whenever he was in school and other students spoke about their fathers. Ms. Grace advised Trevor's teacher that these triggered reminders of his father's absence would cause some of the emotional outbursts and further directed her to strengthen his trust in their relationship by offering him space to share about what he missed about his father. Ms. Grace's approach to attachment therapy not only existed in the interventions within their sessions, but also within the settings where other adults in Trevor's life were present, such as school and home, to ensure he received continual supportive responses that were aligned with attachment therapy and the restructuring of his ability to trust adults.

Attachment-based interventions further the opportunity for clinicians to examine a child's reaction to the therapeutic relationship. Bowlby (1978) proposed that working models are projected onto new relationships and that the experience of making space for this projection provides a focus on how a child's working models affect the child-clinician relationship (Blakely & Dziadosz, 2015). During the therapeutic sessions with Trevor, Ms. Grace would use the space to allow Trevor to openly express statements such as, "How long are you really here for?" or "You're going to leave me just like my daddy did." Ms. Grace knew it was imperative to make space in the sessions to process these statements and explore with Trevor about the impact the loss of his father had on his internal working model of permanency in relationships with adults. After his father's arrest and sentencing, Ms. Grace would note to Trevor's mother that he would start every session with statements like, "When are you leaving me?" and "Why should I tell you? You'll leave like my daddy." Ms. Grace provided a trusting and genuine space for Trevor to share his developmentally appropriate response to anger and loss and would offer feedback in their therapeutic games regarding the transitions he experienced with adults in his life as well as psychoeducation regarding loss that he was unable to control. Trevor was thus able to work toward a new belief system that his father had not abandoned him and that changes in his life with adults who may transition are not leaving him due to his behavior, but rather have circumstances they cannot always control.

A final goal of attachment-based therapy with children who have experienced loss due to incarceration is a central focus on the origin of working models through experiences with childhood primary attachment figures (Blakely & Dziadosz, 2015). This particular focus promotes self-awareness of maladaptive ideas and responses characteristic of an insecure attachment style and ineffective working models. Through Trevor's ability to re-examine why his father was not physically in his life, he was able to address the maladaptive ideas and responses to his fears that adults would leave without becoming withdrawn or anxious when starting new relationships. His relationship with Ms. Grace provided a safe space to practice sharing his responses to his own insecure attachment style and through their use of play-based attachment interventions, Trevor was able to recognize how many adults in his life cared about him, including his father who was incarcerated. This shifted the belief that everyone abandons him, and he did not fear that everyone he met would leave. By Ms. Green assisting Trevor and his mother in recognizing how these beliefs connected to his inner working model of an insecure style that contributed to his emotional distress, Trevor was able to gain a new sense of mastery over his anxiety through a new belief system that he practiced in therapy. In Trevor's therapeutic process, he worked on new skills that promoted reflection on ways to reevaluate and revise working models characteristic of his secure attachment style (Bowlby, 1998).

Addressing Necessary Modifications to Relational-Cultural and Attachment Theory Implementation

Therapists often struggle to identify and assess appropriate clients for treatment. Therefore, while the model works most efficiently for children who present with higher rates of depressive symptoms and have a willingness to engage in the therapeutic process, children who are experiencing stronger symptoms of trauma avoidance and distrust of authoritative figures may struggle to connect to their therapists initially. This can cause critical delays in the application of therapeutic models, such as RCT or attachment theory, that may suggest a time-specific framework. Honoring the process of building a trusting relationship can include expanding the assessment period when the clinician is collecting information on the individual's historical and present relationship to family members. Anxious or depressive symptom arousal and clinical withdrawal can appropriately increase during the assessment period, suggesting that service initiation may increase symptom intensity, especially in circumstances where avoidance is a common form of protection from authoritative figures. Children may have difficulty tolerating these arousal symptoms early in the therapeutic process (Konanur et al., 2015) and, therefore, may struggle adhering to the timetable in the model. Therapeutic flexibility is a necessity for the clinician to employ when implementing RCT frameworks.

Advantages of Relational-Cultural and Attachment Theory Applications for Clinicians

Both relational-cultural and attachment theories recommend experience-dependent learning, which allows for the possibility that persistent, sensitive, and supportive parents may provide some corrective attachment-related experiences for the child.

Both the incarcerated parent and the caregiver who may reside at home can offer a model of care and support that challenges the view that children may hold of caregivers as untrustworthy and of themselves as undeserving of attention and care. In addition, mental health practitioners can use the trusting and safe relationship employed throughout both models to help build the child's understanding of social interactions and provide a safe context in which new relational skills can be developed (Haight et al., 2003). It is important to note that all traumatic events occur within a sociocultural and historical context. More specifically, physical barriers, such as an inability to see a loved one due to financial strain or physical location, reinforce to children impacted by parental incarceration that several systems of oppression, including the medical, mental health, and injustice systems, represent unsafe spaces that hinder healing and recovery. Therefore, even if another person does not acknowledge, address, or name the presence and power of that traumatic event, all traumatic experiences are embedded in a relational context (Kress et al., 2018) that will be difficult for the therapist to undo in their rapport with the child and family. Each model is best understood in the context of relational movement, which is the process of individuals moving safely through connections and disconnections, and back into newly defined and improved connections with others through their own narrative experiences (Comstock et al., 2008).

Reflection Questions

1. Define the terms Relational Therapy and Attachment Theory.
2. How would you incorporate Cultural Responsiveness into your own practice when employing attachment theory with a child experiencing loss due to incarceration?
3. How would you address any bias when assessing attachment barriers?
4. Describe mutual empathy.

References

Arditti, J., & Savla, J. (2005). Parental incarceration and child trauma symptoms in single caregiver homes. *Journal of Child and Family Studies. 24*:3 551–561.

Arditti, J. A., Lambert-Shute, J., & Joest, K. (2003). Saturday morning at the jail: Implications of incarceration for families and children. *Family Relations, 52*(3), 195–204.

Blakely, T. J., & Dziadosz, G. M. (2015). Application of attachment theory in clinical social work. Health & Social Work, *40*(4), 283–289.

Bowlby, J. (1973). *Attachment and loss. Vol. 2: Separation: anxiety and anger*. Basic Books.

Bowlby, J. (1978). *A secure base: Parent-child bureau.*

Bowlby, J. (1998). *A secure base: Parent-child bureau.*

Comfort, M. (2008). Developments and next steps in theorizing the secondary prisonization of families. In *The Palgrave handbook of prison and the family* (pp. 65–79). Palgrave Macmillan.

Comstock, D. L., Hammer, T. R., Strentzsch, J., Cannon, K., Parsons, J., & Salazar II, G. (2008). Relational-cultural theory: A framework for bridging relational, multicultural, and social justice competencies. *Journal of Counseling & Development, 86*(3), 279–287.

Deitz, M. F., Williams, S. L., Rife, S. C., & Cantrell, P. (2015). Examining cultural, social, and self-related aspects of stigma in relation to sexual assault and trauma symptoms. *Violence Against Women, 21*(5), 598–615.

DiLillo, D. (2001). Interpersonal functioning among women reporting a history of childhood sexual abuse: Empirical findings and methodological issues. *Clinical Psychology Review*, *21*(4), 553–576.

Edin, K., Kefalas, M. J., & Reed, J. M. (2004). A peek inside the black box: What marriage means for poor unmarried parents. *Journal of Marriage and the Family, 66*, 1007–1014.

Geller, A., Garfinkel, I., Cooper, C. E., & Mincy, R. B. (2009). Parental Incarceration and Child Well-Being: Implications for Urban Families. *Social Science Quarterly, 90*(5): 1186–1202.

Haight, W. L., Kagle, J. D., & Black, J. E. (2003). Understanding and supporting parent-child relationships during foster care visits: Attachment theory and research. *Social Work*, 48(2), 195–207.

Hairston, C. F. (1998). *Focus on children with incarcerated parents: An overview of the research literature*.

Haskins, N. H., & Appling, B. (2015). Relational-cultural theory and reality therapy: A culturally responsive integrative framework. *Journal of Counseling & Development*, *95*(1), 87–99.

Jordan, J. V. (2010). Relational-cultural therapy. *Handbook of counseling women*, Sage, 63–73.

Konanur, S., Muller, R. T., Cinamon, J. S., Thornback, K., & Zorella, K. (2015). Effectiveness of trauma-focused cognitive behavioral therapy in a community-based program. *Child Abuse and Neglect The International Journal*, *50*, 259–170.

Kress, V. E., Haiyasoso, M., Zoldan, C. A., Headley, J. A., & Trepal, H. (2018). The use of Relational-Cultural Theory in counseling clients who have traumatic stress disorders. *Journal of Counseling & Development*, *96*(1), 106–114. https://doi-org.ezproxy.uno.edu/10.1002/jcad.12182

Mikulincer, M., & Shaver, P. R. (2007). *Attachment in adulthood: Structure, dynamics, and change*. Guilford Press.

Ogle, C. M., Rubin, D. C., & Siegler, I. C. (2013). The impact of the developmental timing of trauma exposure on PTSD symptoms and psychosocial functioning among older adults. *Developmental Psychology*, 49(11), 2191.

Platt, M. G., & Freyd, J. J. (2015). *Psychological Trauma: Theory, Research, Practice, and Policy*, *7*(4), 398–404.

Roy, K. M., & Dyson, O. L. (2005). Gatekeeping in context: Babymama drama and the involvement of incarcerated fathers. *Fathering: A Journal of Theory, Research & Practice about Men as Fathers*, *3*(3), 289–310.

Solomon, A. L., & Zweig, J. (2006). Overview of the issue: Parents in the criminal justice system and its impact on children and families. In *Children of parents in the criminal justice system: Children at risk*.

Sonkin, D. J. (2005). Attachment theory and psychotherapy. *The California Therapist*, 17(1), 68–77.

Sroufe, L. A. (1988). The role of infant-caregiver attachment in development. In J. Belsky & T. Nezworski (Eds.), *Clinical implications of attachment* (pp. 18–38). Lawrence Erlbaum Associates, Inc.

Turney, K. (2014). Stress proliferation across generations? Examining the relationship between parental incarceration and childhood health. *Journal of health and social behavior*, 55(3), 302–319.

Waller, M. R., & Swisher, R. (2006). Fathers' risk factors in fragile families: Implications for "healthy" relationships and father involvement. *Social Problems*, *53*(3), 392–420.

Walsh, K., Fortier, M. A., & DiLillo, D. (2010). Adult coping with childhood sexual abuse: A theoretical and empirical review. *Aggression and violent behavior*, *15*(1), 1–13.

Chapter 8
Mitigation and Advocacy

Over the past several decades, the limited availability of services supporting rehabilitation, such as workforce development, mental health and substance abuse services, or education for incarcerated individuals, is one of the most likely contributors to the high levels of recidivism experienced today. Approximately 75% of people released will return to prison within 3 years because most lack the necessary support to make a successful transition from prison back into their communities. This chapter outlines why the clinical relationship must include mitigation and advocacy practices to support the sustainability of all interventions utilized with parents returning from prison and jail. Without the social worker's or clinician's ability to support re-entry, the family members will risk facing the same cyclical experiences when they return to their communities.

This chapter also describes best practices for clinicians to use when engaging with criminal justice actors (i.e., judges, prosecutors, defense attorneys, employers, or parole officers) and educate readers on how to advocate for alternative sentencing, as well as educational and employment opportunities. This chapter also draws on labeling theory to educate clinicians on how institutionalized social policies reduce the individual to their worst acts by utilizing charged terms with negative connotations like "criminal," "murderer," "rapist," "thief," "drug dealer," "sex offender," or "felon," while describing the importance of language to destigmatize these experiences. A clinician's purposeful and deliberate use of humanistic, holistic language reduces the perpetually punitive associations of the stigmatizing terms commonly used by criminal justice actors.

One case example is used in this chapter: A mother who was at risk of losing full custody of her child after being sentenced to a seven-year prison term for "acting out during a bipolar episode" and how her son describes his aggression, anger, and confusion exhibited during his mother's trial. The case example demonstrates in detail the advocacy actions taken by clinical staff to serve both the families and to support the parents standing trial. The community-based clinician was able to

A. Morgan-Mullane, *An Integrative Approach to Clinical Social Work Practice with Children of Incarcerated Parents*, Essential Clinical Social Work Series,
https://doi.org/10.1007/978-3-031-28823-4_8

utilize mitigation practices highlighting the mother's history of mental health needs, family work, and healing to present to the judge, who dismissed the criminal charges and permitted her to remain under the supervision of the agency and fully address her intergenerational trauma associated with her own father's having gone to prison. During their opportunity to testify on behalf of the mother, the social workers were able to prove the mother's extensive history of PTSD and the intergenerational implications of complex trauma on her son, who required the presence of his mother to heal and restore the functioning of the family.

Alternatives to Incarceration

With the Justice Reinvestment Act, judges were tasked with finding alternatives to incarceration. This act of 2016 was a data-driven approach to reduce corrections spending and redirect savings to other criminal justice strategies that decrease crime and strengthen neighborhoods. This funding promoted more programming as an alternative way of sentencing so that people were offered an opportunity to work, go to school, or get a degree in a variety of fields (technical and non-technical) so that individuals would have an opportunity outside of imprisonment to serve the remainder of their sentence. These alternatives to incarceration also provide measures to ensure that there is no further risk for re-arrest by advocating to end probation early for individuals, waiving individuals' probation costs, or changing their probation from a supervised to unsupervised status.

While there has been a significant increase in alternatives to incarceration programming, it remains vital to clinical practice that therapists aid in bridging the gap between knowledge and practice, as many lawmakers have not incorporated new language, trauma research, or psychosocial learning about rehabilitation into their decisions about sentencing reform (Bagaric et al., 2018). Therefore, clinicians, therapists, and social workers who work with parents and families impacted by the injustice systems must partner with lawmakers to provide these essential clinical offerings during sentencing court hearings. This level of clinical advocacy directly mitigates the incarceration crisis and enhances public safety by placing greater weight on rehabilitation, rather than focusing on incapacitating parents who are presently incarcerated and removed from their families (Bagaric et al., 2018).

Psychosocial Assessments

Presently, American state courts use risk assessment tools in determining sentencing decisions, but these tools often do not have a large impact on sentencing offerings as they are conducted in an underdeveloped manner that is not systematic (Bagaric et al., 2018). In clinical and therapeutic advocacy, clinicians can provide evidence-based trauma findings, symptoms, and diagnoses all centered in experiences associated with incarceration and separation from family. Therapists can also highlight how intergenerational trauma through parental separation and exacerbating symptoms of posttraumatic stress disorder (PTSD) are leading causes of the potential for risk found within a trauma assessment tool, which must be included when offering alternatives to incarceration through court advocacy. It is vital to factor the discussion of the individual's race into sentencing determinations, as it is necessary to consider current decision-making in relation to sentencing in which such tools are not used. Common risk assessments are deficit-based and do not consider the historical and current stressors experienced by the individual that in many instances are rooted in race-based trauma and violence by police and incarceration brutality. It is imperative to stress that race influences many sentencing decisions for a number of reasons, most commonly due to the sentencing judges' internalization of anti-Blackness and racism. These core beliefs about Black Americans stem as a result of a white supremacist legal system that inherently reinforces harsher punishment and sentencing for Black and Brown communities. Therefore, with a psychosocial assessment tool that focuses not only on the strengths of the individual, but also amplifies the trauma experienced within the prison system, alternative programming offers opportunity for healing and rehabilitation for families.

Black Americans are incarcerated at more than five times the rate at which white Americans are imprisoned. Bagaric et al. (2018) found that within an especially wide-ranging study, "77,000 [incarcerated people were surveyed] who received sentences [and found that] Black defendants are sentenced to prison terms that are 12% longer than prison terms issued to white individuals who have committed the same crimes and have identical criminal histories" (p. 55). Similarly, a study issued for the United States Bureau of Justice Statistics and the United States Department of Justice Working Group on Racial Disparity reported that the federal jurisdiction between 2005 and 2012 saw judges executing prison sentences on Black men that were nearly 5–10% longer than those enforced on white offenders for similar offenses (Bagaric et al., 2018). Between 2005 and 2012, the court system had extensive decision over sentencing because in 2005 the United States Supreme Court maintained in *Booker v. United States* that the Federal Sentencing Guidelines were "advisory rather than mandatory" (Bagaric et al., 2018). As such, the pervasiveness of racial bias in sentencing has proved to traumatically affect Black and Brown communities during the time of legal decision-making. Accordingly, clinicians working with families impacted by mass incarceration must utilize their clinical expertise to include trauma assessments that reinforce the need for alternatives to incarceration. To combat the disproportionate number of Black parents taken from their families, mental health practitioners working with children of incarcerated parents must center legal advocacy and mitigation practices as a primary goal of the treatment plan of each child and their parent.

Mitigation Partnerships and Advocacy

Clinicians working with children of incarcerated parents must research and partner with affiliated organizations and employers, which can include the Departments of Parole and Probation, Pretrial Supervision, and the State's Attorney and Public

Defender's Offices, among others. The expansive clinical practice for clinicians working with children of incarcerated parents should also engage with funding opportunities to provide more permanent positions for clinical mitigation practices, as many clinicians often feel as though they do not have enough time for research and legal partnership. Therefore, the development of this role proves to be critical in the practice of employing therapeutic advocacy and the success rate of reducing a parent's sentence. These practices are crucial to sustaining the mental health of the parent and their child, which gives individuals direct access to better mental healthcare and legal justice through alternative sentencing options.

Mitigation Illustration: Rhonda's[1] Story

The following narrative is an illustration of Children of Promise, NYC, a community-based organization working specifically with children of incarcerated parents. The interview with the incarcerated parent demonstrates the need to consider one's own trauma history during sentencing and the alternative for healing that is essential to the individual's opportunity for growth and wellness, as well as their family member's opportunity for the same experience of intergenerational healing. The example provides clinicians with the necessary considerations to present to judges and district attorneys as programming adjustments were made to adhere to all legal oversight within the sentencing decision.

Presentation of Trauma History

Rhonda is a 33-year-old female with an extensive history of complex trauma related to physical, emotional, and psychological abuse. She suffers from symptoms of chronic PTSD, including hostility, hypervigilance, social isolation, self-destructive behaviors, flashbacks, fear, severe anxiety, distrust of others, loss of interest and pleasure in activities, guilt, loneliness, insomnia, nightmares, emotional detachment, and unwanted thoughts. Rhonda reports that she experienced physical abuse and witnessed domestic violence and substance misuse in her home at age 5, which caused Rhonda to feel unsafe and led to her to stay away from her home, when she began to associate with older individuals in her neighborhood without adult supervision.

During her psychosocial assessment while incarcerated, the social work team at the jail setting diagnosed Rhonda with Post Traumatic Stress Disorder Chronic (ICD-10 Code F43.12) (World Health Organization, 2004).

They identified her psychosocial stressors as a significant history of incarceration, loss of her father due to a life sentence of imprisonment, loss of her biological mother due to substance abuse, removal from the family at the age of 12 due to child

[1] Pseudonyms are used in this chapter to preserve confidentiality.

abuse and neglect, multiple placements in foster care, and being a victim of community violence.

At this time, Rhonda reported that she was robbed and stabbed at age 12, which led to her having an emergency splenectomy. This highly intensive procedure led to Rhonda sustaining both physical and emotional trauma. Rhonda further reported that she no longer felt safe in her own community. Rhonda lost her father due to a life sentence of incarceration and lost her mother due to chronic substance misuse. After Rhonda sustained a medical trauma, she was placed in foster care, at which time she was abruptly separated from her younger brother for 2 years as they were both placed in different foster homes. Rhonda attributed the devastation of losing her brother while in foster care as a direct correlation to the anger that she carried when he was first arrested at age 16. At this time, Rhonda was without family, guidance, or support, which exacerbated her emotional state of pain, loss, and depression.

From the ages of 16 to 19, Rhonda reported experiencing feelings of confusion, loss, and anger while incarcerated without any support shown from her biological family. In contrast, the meaningful relationships that Rhonda stated have had a positive impact on her life have been her relationship with her stepson Jeremiah and husband Jay. Rhonda reports having met them once she was released from prison, and they have remained as significant figures in her life as well as her only identified sources of strength and life. Rhonda stated that she was never able to receive any form of therapeutic care, which would have encouraged her ability to feel more confident about her life choices. While incarcerated, Rhonda also experienced significant violence, which reinforced and intensified her PTSD symptoms of paranoia and a fear of trusting others. Prior to her work with Children of Promise, NYC, Rhonda confirmed, she was unable to engage in therapy due to being fearful of authoritative figures as she was severely neglected, abused, and abandoned her entire life.

Presently, Rhonda has engaged in therapeutic treatment with her assigned clinician, with whom she has been able to speak over the phone and has met in person for therapeutic sessions while she was on Rikers Island. During these sessions, Rhonda continues to bravely explore and disclose her trauma history of significant violence and abuse that she witnessed and endured by family members, foster care parents, community gang members, and those who were incarcerated during Rhonda's previous incarceration. Rhonda has expressed feeling very hopeful that she will be able to continue her intensive trauma-responsive care if able to return home. Additionally, Rhonda has also expressed feeling optimistic about her ability to engage in the healing process for her own psychological and psychiatric growth, as well as the support that her husband and stepson provide.

Clinical Advocacy

Rhonda was receiving intensive trauma-focused cognitive behavioral therapy and motivational interviewing twice a week with her assigned individual psychotherapist. In these sessions, she was able to identify the current post-traumatic stress symptoms from which she suffers. This therapy has ensured that she does not re-experience the traumatic events from her history and supported her in maintaining impulse control. She was also receiving twice-weekly structural family therapy with her assigned family therapist to enhance communication within her family system and maintain familial connections with her son and husband. The agency's chief psychiatrist has managed any psychotropic medications to support her management of physical and emotional trauma symptoms.

Therefore, with all the extensive clinical services she was receiving, she requested that she be considered for closer placement to her clinical and medical outpatient mental health clinic, as well as where her family resides as their participation in her treatment was instrumental. The clinical team advocated through mitigation practices that she be placed at a closer correctional facility so that therapeutic services may continue with the relationship she was presently strengthening with stepson, husband, and therapists. CPNYC provided van services to ensure there was no disruption in her weekly clinical visits from the mental health team who had been providing her psychiatric care.

CPNYC had provided these services to Rhonda prior to her most recent incarceration, and they advocated to maintain these therapeutic practices if she is considered for placement at a closer facility or early release for alternative sentencing. The organization's services are rooted in evidence-based practice and curated by the Cure Violence Model, for adults affected by the violence, including traumas associated with incarceration (Cure Violence Global, 2021). Trained Licensed Clinical Master's in Social Work facilitators, psychiatrists, and psychologists work individually to recognize how trauma and violence affect the individual's physiology, cognitive processes, and social and behavioral interactions.

As a program, CPNYC clinicians assess the individual's ecological structure to evaluate the contextual factors that impact the transmission of systemic stress on the family which contributes to the continuum of violence (Cure Violence Global, n.d.). The individual and group mechanisms that provide violent pathways into an individual's life can be contributed by several factors that vary from family to family.

To create the most comprehensive and holistic experience, CPNYC partnered with several alternative-to-incarceration programs to help with Rhonda's psychiatric recovery. These specific partnerships shift the dynamics of therapy into group work by connecting community members committed to transforming the direction of their lives as well as cleansing the violence from their communities. These individuals have experienced and participated in violence firsthand. Together, the group is able to create a greater understanding of how violence has affected their mental health as well as their social interactions. The individual, family, and group work are able to support one another in their own recovery, and Rhonda was able to cultivate change in her immediate community. The group works together to anticipate where violence will occur, intervene before violence has a chance to erupt, and supply supportive resources to families affected by violence. This direct connection is not only healing for the individual, but it is also essential to cultivating a change in social norms.

The model for trauma-responsive psychiatric services in conjunction with group and direct community practice creates a comprehensive approach to resilience, which encompasses culture, place, religion, family, and the law. Overwhelming evidence suggests that the family domain is a critical protective and promotional step toward individual and intergenerational resilience. When trying to change community-level contextual factors, it is important to also support families, which helps support the larger social environment while working to change family functioning.

When a child loses a parent to incarceration, they experience disruption in their emotional health and well-being. For this reason, mental health services are a critical component of the program model to support the entire family when a parent is facing re-entry into their community. Roughly 55% of incarcerated men and 73% of incarcerated women have mental illness, yet only about 33% of this population receive any sort of mental healthcare. This lapse in care can be deeply scarring to someone struggling with a mental illness (James & Glaze, 2006).

In keeping with this fact, the agency legally advocated in court that, to continue their services for Rhonda, she should be placed at a facility closer to their outpatient Article 31 behavioral health clinic where she would be able to utilize mental health services as a primary source of support. Two days a week, a team of psychiatrists, social workers, and psychologists provides the following services using an evidence-based and trauma-informed lens:

- Individual and family psychotherapy
- Partnership with the agency's case management program
- Re-entry employment and academic goals and objectives offered throughout each session

The services provided to each family are based on an understanding of the prevalence of traumatic stress in their community, and the therapeutic models they apply are proven to be effective for the specific needs of children with imprisoned parents. The licensed social workers and psychiatrists are specially trained in the following modalities, among others, that best support the behaviors and symptoms associated with traumatic experiences:

- Trauma-focused cognitive behavioral therapy
- Cognitive behavioral therapy
- Relational therapy
- Narrative therapy
- Mindfulness practices

Rhonda's clinical team presented this programming and advocacy lens of alternative sentencing and closer placement to her family during the time of her sentencing. The team reported that upon re-entry into her own community, she would face psychological and structural barriers that would feel heightened due to her PTSD diagnosis, her family's low socioeconomic status, and the effects of the trauma of incarceration. Her involvement with their comprehensive mental health services that work in tandem with their case management program offered a well-rounded support system to assist Rhonda with financial stability and to secure housing, stable employment, and comprehensive medical and psychiatric care. Without mental health treatment addressing both her emotional and concrete needs, the team explained to the judges, further incarceration and the traumatic living conditions of jail or prison would worsen her symptoms. The team conveyed that if they offered her full membership into their program while incarcerated, the opportunity to meet with her weekly would decrease both her likelihood of re-arrest and overall costs to the jail and prison system in the long term. Their well-rounded rehabilitative services that specialize in re-entry post-incarceration would provide Rhonda with the most healing and permanent solution to her psychiatric condition and her previous incarceration experiences—a goal that an increase of time spent incarcerated would never be able to accomplish.

The judges listened to the extensive overview of psychiatric services that would be able to detect and interrupt Rhonda's psychiatric and physiological responses to trauma, identify and treat high-risk cognitions surrounding violence, and mobilize change within her individual behaviors. The judges then initially granted the request for placement closer to her family be considered so that her extensive treatment could be provided throughout the week. Rhonda was able to receive individualized trauma-focused psychodynamic therapy and family psychotherapy as her family was able to attend weekly sessions during each visit with a social worker from CPNYC. Additionally, Rhonda was granted early release and was able to attend a trauma intervention group upon her release. Finally, in partnership with community-based alternative-to-incarceration programs focused on employment and education, Rhonda was able to continue her therapeutic healing process by contributing to her community through her role as a credible messenger, which is someone who has direct experience with what others are presently walking through in the program. She would work with a community-based organization to assess risk, intervene to stop violence, and contribute to a change of police practices within the community.

Intergenerational Trauma: Rhonda's Family Voice

During Rhonda's sentencing hearing, excerpts were read from several reports and assessments conducted by the clinical team. Rhonda's stepson asked to read his letter to the judge in which he wrote about his anger, anxiety, and worry about her well-being every day. School reports suggested his decline in grades and focus in specific classes were due to difficulty in paying attention after his stepmother's arrest and incarceration. Rhonda's stepson expressed to the judge, "Having to visit my mom in jail only makes me more angry to know she can't come home with me at the end of our visit. I feel like I have a wound that can't heal until she is home, but yet I'm expected to perform at school like everything is fine and will only get punished if I show how I really feel. I need my mom home so I can be okay."

CPNYC's mitigation efforts included a comprehensive overview of how their services are uniquely tailored to children who have shared similar experiences like Rhonda's stepson with well-rounded support, especially within their legal advocacy program. The clinicians showcased how they first assess the primary needs in terms of health, financial stability, and support systems for each child, their present caretaker, and their incarcerated parent. Within the assessment phase, they are sure to highlight the strengths of the family and indicate potential risk as systemic barriers to formerly incarcerated adults. New language is utilized so that individuals feel as though the incarceration experience is not one of blaming toward the parent. Throughout the planning phase of the program, the clinicians also employ language that validates and affirms the family. In many legal settings, parents, adults, and children are referred to as "felon," "convict," "inmate," and "criminal." Therefore, they assure the family and family's legal team that the parent's name will always be used to demand that the humanity of the person be seen throughout the course of their partnered clinical work together. Clinicians will train lawyers, judges, and parole officers in the same practices to guarantee that the personhood of the parent is centered at all times. The agency informed the judge that after a list of goals and needs are co-created by the parent and their personal clinician and family clinician, the advocates oversee the entire family's needs in the following areas:

1. Housing stability: Coming from a housing-first perspective, house advocates ensure that our families have stable housing at the start of their relationship as a foundation to develop a new start after release from incarceration.
2. Medical coordination: The medical social work advocates ensure that appointments are scheduled, prescriptions are financially accessible if needed, specialist providers are found, and the parents have accompaniment to all of their medical appointments to prevent hospitalization and promote preventive healthcare and overall wellness, should this be a request by the parent.
3. Mental health coordination: The family coordinators provide in-house, person-centered, and trauma-responsive psychotherapy and psychiatry through individual, family, and group sessions. These family coordinators manage appointments and ensure clear communication between mental healthcare providers and families.
4. Career services: Career counselors work individually with previously incarcerated family members to evaluate their strengths and discover their own personal desired employment or educational programs and gainful employment within the first 3 months of their release.
5. Financial management: Banking systems and materials are reviewed within the member's individual family circumstances to ensure stability in the member's ability to open up a bank account without any systemic barrier or challenge to embolden parents to pay their bills, rent, and other living expenses according to their means.
6. Legal aid: Through the organization's partnerships with non-profit legal aid agencies city-wide, they are able to link the families with the necessary services to address any legal needs they may have with parole, family court, or any other legal necessities.

Due to the length of Rhonda's incarceration, her previous trauma history, the clinical work throughout her incarceration, and her stepson's appeal, the judge granted Rhonda the alternative-to-incarceration program presented by CPNYC throughout her appeal. The agency and Rhonda agreed that all healing components of the program's model and design presented throughout the mitigation practices would reflect her own desire for a journey of trauma recovery, her family's rehabilitation from prior trauma of losing one another, and her own path to unpacking her intergenerational trauma that she committed to "stopping now with [her] stepson."

Reflection Questions

1. Is clinical advocacy relevant for all child clients, not just those impacted by parental incarceration? If so, why?
2. Name other mental health-based stigmatizing terms often used in the clinical profession. How does this impact how you see your client?
3. Do you feel assessments should be changed to reflect client's assets and strengths?
4. Identify where you could employ legal mitigation practices in your work. What barriers might be involved in this process?

References

Bagaric, M., Wolf, G., & Rininger, W. (2018). Mitigating America's mass incarceration crisis without compromising community protection: Expanding the role of rehabilitation in sentencing. *Lewis & Clark Law Review*, *22*(1), 1–60

Cure Violence Global. (n.d.). *Cure Violence Global.* https://cvg.org. Accessed 15 Mar 2023.

Cure Violence Global. (2021). *The evidence of effectiveness*. https://cvg.org/impact/. Accessed 24 Feb 2023.

James, D. J., & Glaze, L. E. (2006, September). Mental health problems of prison and jail inmates. *Bureau of justice statistics special report.* Office of Justice Programs, U.S. Department of Justice. https://www.ojp.gov/ncjrs/virtual-library/abstracts/mental-health-problems-prison-and-jail-inmates. Accessed 9 Mar 2023.

World Health Organization. (2004). ICD-10: International statistical classification of diseases and related health problems: Tenth revision, 2nd ed. World Health Organization. https://apps.who.int/iris/handle/10665/42980. Accessed 24 Feb 2023.

Part III
Enhancing Practice Through Supervision and Training

Chapter 9
Supervision and the Therapeutic Alliance: Critical Consciousness and Anti-racist Clinical Training and Undoing

Therapists, supervisors, social work schools, training institutes, and agencies rely on the simple and brief utilization of an assessment tool or portion of a biopsychosocial assessment to explore the impact of race, culture, and institutions on a person's clinical experience. Children and adolescents impacted by the loss of a parent to incarceration experience layers of trauma often rooted in racial bias and ongoing narratives of discrimination, which reinforce feelings of shame and stigma in relation to that parental loss. Therefore, this chapter highlights the use of critical consciousness and cultural humility as a continual and integrative approach to clinical assessment and therapeutic treatment planning. Critical consciousness (CC) encourages the clinician to take a more active role in understanding the institutional and societal effects on clients and to work to enact changes in those realms. Whereas clinical social work is traditionally thought to be a micro-level practice where the emphasis is on the therapeutic relationship, CC encourages social workers to consider the critical interaction between the institutional effects of mass incarceration and the clinical dimension. Brief examples illustrate the parallel process that often exists in this situation for the child, family, and clinician to build a closer therapeutic rapport that builds trust and healing throughout the remainder of their partnership.

Mosley et al. (2021) describes the detrimental effects of racial trauma on Black people, which requires the need for therapeutic interventions to facilitate the resistance to and prevention of structural racism within the clinical profession. Mosley et al. (2021) highlights how critical consciousness is one example of a culturally responsive intervention, as it is often seen as a requirement of resistance and liberation (Prilleltensky, 2003, 2008). When working with children of incarcerated parents, clinicians must employ practices that offer core values within a racial justice framework. This is because the layers of racism, oppression, and anti-Blackness experienced by children and families impacted by the carceral system continually magnify racial trauma as a primary source of pain when addressing their healing through a therapeutic relationship. Clinicians, practices, and educators must ensure

A. Morgan-Mullane, *An Integrative Approach to Clinical Social Work Practice with Children of Incarcerated Parents*, Essential Clinical Social Work Series,
https://doi.org/10.1007/978-3-031-28823-4_9

that their training and supervision offer tools to address racism and systems of oppression not only within all systems experienced by the child and family, but also within the mental healthcare experience.

An Anti-racist Continuing Education Clinical Training Program

An example of an anti-racist clinical training program for clinicians working with children of incarcerated parents is Children of Promise, NYC (CPNYC). CPNYC was the first to establish this community practice orientation using evidence-informed treatment modalities with the specific population of children of incarcerated parents. Over the course of our 10-year research, clinical practice, and curriculum development, we have shaped our training to address trauma symptoms exhibited by children and adolescents. CPNYC's research highlights how similar symptomatology—depression, anger, isolating and self-harming behaviors, cognitive distortions, and escalated symptoms of physical distress—is reported by children impacted by parental incarceration. Therefore, their trauma-focused modality is applicable to the treatment of the childhood trauma of parental incarceration, as it is to other forms of childhood trauma. Their training explores the psychological manifestation of trauma symptoms related to parental incarceration and lays the groundwork for the implementation of CPNYC's community-based treatment modality.

CPNYC has developed six-hour courses and two-hour courses (two of each) for Continuing Education Units (CEU) accreditation and licensure hours for all mental health practitioners in NYC. Its training institute courses cover efficacious practices for working with children of incarcerated parents, including the use of trauma-focused, evidence-based treatment modalities in responding to parental incarceration as a major traumatic event in the lives of children. The lead trainers provide audiences with a comprehensive discussion around the historical oppression, specifically of children of incarcerated parents, by defining anti-Blackness within the realm of social services from micro, mezzo, and macro practice levels to enhance therapeutic relationships for practitioners treating children of incarcerated parents. Furthermore, all their courses utilize an anti-oppressive lens by contextualizing present-day parental incarceration within the political history of mass incarceration in the United States.

CPNYC's clinical trainers and experts expand on the dialogue regarding children of incarcerated parents by recognizing that the phenomenon of hyper-incarceration is associated with conscious and unconscious racially harmful practices within clinical practice that affect children of incarcerated parents. Contextual factors like structural racism compound the impacts of mass incarceration on children and have the potential to create inherent racial biases in clinicians and the general population alike. Both courses explore and recommend solutions to dismantle oppressive clinical practices in therapeutic spaces and offer the audience training opportunities to draw out their own unconscious racist beliefs and practices that fail to account for the historical and contextual needs and issues specific to populations affected by mass incarceration.

Through its integration of the micro-level clinical interventions, along with the mezzo- and macro-level identification of the historical and present-day oppression of parental incarceration, current courses take a comprehensive approach to identifying the trauma of parental incarceration and best practices in treating children of incarcerated parents. The goals and objectives of its current training model allows for participants to:

1. Understand historical oppression and mass incarceration through the lens of anti-Blackness in clinical practice on a micro, mezzo, and macro level.
2. Identify parental incarceration as a newly recognized form of trauma and the post-traumatic symptoms exhibited by children of incarcerated parents.
3. Speak to the efficacy of evidence-based and evidence-informed treatment models, including trauma-focused cognitive behavioral therapy, trauma systems therapy, narrative therapy, and community psychiatry as best practices for clinical treatment with children of incarcerated parents.
4. Develop an increased capacity to interrupt the profound impact of mass incarceration on children, families, and communities and identify the skills necessary to target and dismantle anti-Blackness in clinical practice.
5. Demonstrate an understanding of the impact of mass incarceration on clinical services, supervision, and social work and mental health education programs.

Throughout the specialized training courses, clinicians learn to identify racial trauma, which is also described as race-based traumatic stress, or psychological, emotional, and physical injury from experiencing real and perceived racism (Bryant-Davis & Ocampo, 2007; Carter, 2007). Racial trauma is narratively defined by children of incarcerated parents as a primary trauma and accounts for experiences of racism directly associated with racial comments or messages made by the broader society regarding their parents. These accounts can include such overt statements as "Your dad/mom must be a dangerous person" as an assumption that people who are incarcerated are inherently dangerous. Examples of racial trauma in overt language also include children's examples of social workers assuming their parent "was a drug dealer" or "did drugs," which led to their incarceration and labeled them as a "neglectful" or "abusive parent." Covert examples of racial trauma experienced by children of incarcerated parents include exclusion based on assumptions of racial inferiority, such as "You're going to follow in your parent's footsteps" or referring to a child's parent as a "criminal," "felon," "inmate," "drug dealer," or "abusive" or "negligent." Children of incarcerated parents also report experiences unique to racial trauma, which include interpersonal discrimination and harassment (Mosley et al., 2021), as well as institutional and systemic racism, such as personal traumatic experiences with systemic excessive use of force by the police (Bryant-Davis & Ocampo, 2007; Carter, 2007). Racial trauma reflects similar symptoms of post-traumatic stress disorder, which is conveyed through re-experiencing trauma, avoidance, arousal, and negative mood and cognitions (Carter, 2007; Williams et al.,

2018). Clinicians working therapeutically with families impacted by the injustice system will need to utilize a framework of clinical practice that is embedded with unpacking racial trauma and understanding parental incarceration as a primary trauma, in addition to tools to undo the clinicians' own racial bias in relation to their own beliefs about individuals within the injustice system.

Culture-Based Countertransference Defined

Stampley (2008) introduces the term *culture-based countertransference* (CBC) as what is conceptualized by clinicians to be culturally maintained "assumptions, values, attitudes, standards, worldviews, and intergenerational messages along with their feelings and thoughts about clients" (p. 40). When clinicians are cognizant of their CBCs, they can improve their recognition of feelings, thoughts, emotional responses, values, and attitudes that affect the therapeutic process. This undoing and naming process within the supervision setting allows for greater depth in the assessment process, treatment planning, and overall clinical relationship. More explicitly, when clinicians who seek anti-racist and anti-oppressive supervision recognize how CBCs influence the therapeutic process, they are able to address the necessary changes within themselves, as well as the therapeutic relationship to ensure the child, family, or adult is able to have their own narrative of community and culture at the center of the treatment.

Culture-Based Countertransference: Utilizing Critical Consciousness in Clinical Supervision

Critical consciousness, also known as conscientization or sociopolitical development (Mosley et al., 2021), is an intervention to diminish, prevent, and resist racial trauma (Prilleltensky, 2003). Critical consciousness can also be described as an individual's ability to become present and aware of the stressors and barriers in their lives through their lived experiences and sociopolitical environments to which they respond with resistance and liberation as they begin a process of personal and communal healing. Examples of this liberation and action through a framework of critical consciousness can be shown through a response to individual and systemic racism by engaging in actions such as Black racial justice activism and community organizing as a direct response to their critical reflection (Diemer et al., 2006).

Within clinical supervision, supervisors teach and train clinical strategies to demonstrate critical consciousness for practitioners working with children of incarcerated parents. Methods of this practice, as displayed through supervision, occur when a clinician is taught how to effectively partner therapeutically with a family and join in their own advocacy efforts to bring greater awareness of the racially driven traumatic implications of losing a loved one to the injustice system. Supervisors who apply CC to clinical practice support practitioners identifying group healing modalities rooted in activism for children and families. This is determined through the creation of support groups for both children and parents, who then speak out at community forums and local government gatherings. Each collective conversation by the creation of these support groups or advisory boards is designed by the children and parents themselves. This empowerment process of sharing their unique experience is then used to design not only their own treatment plan and personal goals but also to encourage re-shaping of programming for community-based initiatives specifically established for children of incarcerated parents. Within the parallel process of clinicians and children developing critical consciousness, individuals and collectives can work strategically and systemically toward healing and protection from racial trauma (Mosley et al., 2021).

Discussing Race in Clinical Practice

Addressing the interpersonal relationship between the therapist and child and/or family is essential when exploring race within supervision practices. With the utilization of critical consciousness and culture-based countertransference, the clinical supervisor encourages the clinician to explore how race can be both a silent and loud participant in therapeutic sessions. In social psychological literature, racial anxiety refers to the concerns that often arise before and during interracial interactions (Godsil & Richardson, 2017). Children of incarcerated parents who identify as people of color report experiencing racial anxiety when they worry that they will be subjected to discriminatory treatment. In mental health-based settings, children have reported experiences such as, "When I shared with my school counselor that my dad was in jail, she asked why and when I didn't tell her, she told my principal she wanted to call ACS. She is a white woman." Thirteen-year-old Tianna[1] describes feelings of fear that are rooted in encounters with white authoritative figures as she has regularly "been punished for beliefs about myself or my family that are clearly racist. [The counselor] wanted me to open up for it and when I shared, I got in trouble, and my family is at risk now."

Racial anxiety can influence behaviors and judgments in ways that contribute to significant and unwarranted racial disparities as white clinicians respond harmfully to information provided within therapeutic sessions. If these racial biases, both cognitive and emotional, go unaddressed within supervision, the continual process of cyclical harm is detrimental to the child's and family's healing process. White-bodied clinicians need to unpack their racialized responses, communication styles, and treatment goals through a supervision process. A white-bodied therapist can maintain white power and privilege that can only exist in an unexamined individual

[1] Pseudonyms are used in this chapter to preserve confidentiality.

who avoids introspection and reflection (Bate & Ng, 2021). It requires a level of inquiry often provided by a supervisor who can name the harm even in the absence of both conscious and implicit racial bias. Within implicit racial bias, racial anxiety can aggravate interracial dynamics in ways that create significant mistrust in the therapeutic alliance (Godsil & Richardson, 2017). Mental health practitioners are professionally and personally socialized into a specific way of thinking and acting toward communities of color and those who are in close proximity to Blackness as their training curriculum often positions them to see themselves as experts in the lives of others. Culture-based countertransference combats the belief of being more knowledgeable and calls out whiteness as a barrier to therapeutic harmony with children and families impacted by mass incarceration.

Critical Consciousness and Culture-Based Countertransference in Supervision

Clinical supervisors who impart knowledge and clinical application of critical consciousness and culture-based countertransference will offer clinicians necessary exploration of how traumatizing the effects of anti-Black violence are on the children and families impacted by the carceral system. This growth of knowledge from the clinician will strengthen the accountable space created in the therapeutic setting and can be effectively executed through practices of critical consciousness and culture-based countertransference. Freud (1910) conceptualized countertransference as the clinician's conflict-laden unconscious and defensive reactions to the individual's transference that is essential to address and be worked through in an effort to not cause harm to the therapeutic relationship (Stampley, 2008). Without proper supervision to undo these cultural responses and belief systems held by the clinician, many clinicians remain unaware of what is unconsciously brought up, expressed, or experienced through their own countertransferences because countertransferences are so endemic. Clinical literature and training readily explore the child's or adult's transferences but rarely refer to clinicians' countertransferences toward racially based frameworks (Stampley, 2008). Race, racial trauma, and systemic racial oppression must be taken into account when clinicians' countertransferences are discussed and explored.

Racial Trauma and Children of Incarcerated Parents

As several children share narratives of directly experiencing police brutality, the clinician is responsible for introducing into discussion that racial anxiety about police encounters and implicit association of deviance, aggression, and criminality with Black people result in a disproportionate use of police force against Black individuals and community members (Bate & Ng, 2021). If these experiences are not recognized and named during the intake assessment phase of the therapeutic relationship and throughout the clinical work when unpacking trauma, the clinician is building a fractured relationship with the child. When assessing trauma, supervisors must guide their clinicians on how to name negative police encounters as the cause of trauma symptoms, which include a heightened sense of stress, anxiety, and trauma (Bate & Ng, 2021). Because the intersection between race and mental wellness has often been overlooked, supervisors can instruct clinicians to mitigate symptoms of distress and racial trauma by implementing critical consciousness as a primary clinical intervention that amplifies the child's lived experience with the violence they witnessed from police and systemic racism they continue to endure and then identify sources of power they can identify with for communal healing and political accountability. The breakdown of trust between the clinician and child is addressed when the clinician unpacks their own unaddressed racial anxiety and desire to be trusted by the child or family. Clinical supervisors can further identify the aftereffects of racial violence that mass incarceration inflicts upon those who are not direct victims, such as the children, families, and communities, and how this impedes the initial phase of engagement in the therapeutic relationship. Thus, clinicians can declare racial violence associated with mass incarceration as a primary trauma requiring appropriate policy response from law enforcement, healthcare, business, education, and the media as an intervention embedded in critical consciousness.

Processing of culture-based countertransference challenges clinicians to be aware of the power they have and how this power is experienced in relation to those they work with. This practice requires intentional and ongoing self-reflection on one's perception of self and others throughout treatment grounded in the construct of social justice (Parke & Clarke-Stewart, 2001). Supervisors can encourage the clinician to take a more active role in understanding the institutional and societal effects on children of incarcerated parents and to work to make changes in those realms. Whereas clinical practice is traditionally thought to be a micro-level practice where the emphasis is on the therapeutic relationship, critical consciousness encourages clinicians and practitioners to consider the critical interaction between the institutional effects of mass incarceration in the clinical dimension. Supervisors support clinicians in their own undoing of how they were professionally and personally socialized into a specific way of thinking and acting. Culture is also a silent participant in every therapeutic session (Stampley, 2008). Clinical insight gleaned from CBC can deepen clinicians' awareness of relationship dynamics and provide valuable information about the therapeutic process.

Mental health practitioners' worldviews operate from a culture-based set of assumptions about how a problem is to be identified, understood, and resolved (Green, 1982; Foster, 1999). Therefore, the clinical supervisor's primary goal in culture-based countertransference is to address how the clinician can actively combat the same conscious and unconscious practices of stereotyping and ethnocentrism as the general public, regardless of their training in their graduate curriculum and programming (Bloombaum et al., 1968). Stampley (2008) suggested that since there has not been significant documentation of a paradigm shift in how clinicians actively engage in their own process of undoing racism, people receiving therapy still report degrees of racial stereotyping and ethnocentrism in their experiences with the general public or in mental health professional practices. Clinical professionals' racial bias will require ongoing supervision as an active goal for continual change on this front of therapeutic practice.

The commitment to supervision grounded in CC and CBC for practitioners working with children and families impacted by parental incarceration centers the child and family's authentic narrative and racial trauma as the focal point of treatment. The clinical relationship becomes less about a clinician imposing a certain clinical treatment on an individual through their own unconscious bias and white privilege lens, but rather on the child, caregiver, and clinician co-creating an appropriate treatment based on the child's expressed needs. The clinician then enthusiastically supports this type of exploration, which is foundational to CC and CBC values. All individuals raised in a society with a centuries-long history of racism will intrinsically carry unconscious biases and attitudes that influence one's thinking and behavior in complex ways. If clinicians do not acknowledge that they have these beliefs and carry them into interpersonal exchanges in therapy, then they will continue to bring these behaviors into clinical spaces and continually blame the individual for not forming trusting relationships and complying with the treatment process.

Case Illustration of CC and CBC in Application

The following case example is an interview with a social worker and their supervisor at a community-based practice that serves children of incarcerated parents. The social worker, who identifies as an Asian-American cisgender male, participated in a 12-month supervision process with their clinical supervisor, who identifies as a cisgender female and a white adjacent Latina. The supervisor devoted 90 minutes a week to individual supervision grounded in CC and CBC principles. The social worker and supervisor summarized the stages of self-examination that occurred throughout their work together. The social work supervisor stated:

> There are often three stages of initial exploration used to start clinical supervision established in critical consciousness and culture-based countertransference: (1) social workers' life history information; (2) their own clinical understanding of the counseling processes (i.e., assessment, goals, interventions or treatments, termination, and referrals); and (3) clinical judgments across the therapeutic process. When I had [the clinician] begin the first phase of the supervision, he expressed it was new for him to share more personally about his own culture and upbringing as a useful tool for his own clinical practice. We began to explore how his history impacted his desire to go into social work but that culturally, due to his proximity to whiteness, he upheld certain beliefs about treatment protocols that were more rigid and less exploratory as a result of his social work education and training. I found in our work together that he was able to name the oppressive nature of educational training and how this kept him from knowing much about mass incarceration and racially-based violence in the community he was serving. When we reached the third phase of the clinical

> supervision, he was more readily able to access the inherent racialized bias and judgements he felt he was indoctrinated with as a result of a lack of understanding the criminal justice system prior to working at our agency.

The social worker supervised through CC and CBC affirmed the three phases of their structured sessions over the course of his first 12 months within the agency. The clinician shared that this particular focus of supervision aided in his own undoing of racial bias and held him more accountable for increased learning about mass incarceration and the greater impact it had on the community as a whole:

> When I first started, I felt confident in my skills. I didn't realize until starting supervision with Rebecca that I had been fully indoctrinated with my own relationship to white saviorism. I thought my passion for the work was enough. But when I began feeling disconnected in sessions with the kids who spoke about police brutality, I realized they could also feel my disconnection as well. It was the first kind of supervision I experienced where I was asked about my own narrative and how this informed what I was walking into each session with. I knew I had unconscious racial bias, but I didn't realize how deep this bias then informed my expectations of the therapeutic relationship. I was able to recognize how my own proximity to whiteness permitted me to have many safe experiences with police and authoritative figures throughout my education, so when I'd have judgments about a child's behavior, I didn't realize I was dismissing their lived experience of racial oppression. Rebecca challenged me to name my own experiences, my social work educational experiences, and re-examine how these beliefs have kept me from forming trusting relationships with clients. When I began to shift, I could tell the kids actually believed my energy and my flexibility and commitment to social injustice became more present in and out of sessions with the families. It was really powerful.

Clinicians who actively engage in CC and CBC express feeling more connected relationally to the therapeutic process as there is an honoring that trust must be earned and not expected to be given. The illustrations above offer clinicians the deeper insight into the humility and openness that is required to strengthen the therapeutic bond which in turn provides further success in therapeutic outcomes for the individual and clinician.

Reflection Questions

1. Can you define Critical Consciousness and was this taught in your social work education?
2. For those who supervise, or those who wish to become supervisors, what do you feel you must embody to help your supervisee unpack bias?
3. Where do you feel training programs struggle to highlight addressing clinical harm when discussing race, gender, abilities, etc.?
4. Where you taught or guided in exploration of how mass incarceration is traumatically impacting many communities that social workers serve? If no, why do you feel this conversation is absent in supervision?
5. How do you hope to integrate these outlined practices into your supervision process both as a supervisor and supervisee?

References

Bate, K. A., & Ng, E. S. (2021). Whiteness in academia, time to listen, and moving beyond White fragility. *Equality, Diversity and Inclusion: An International Journal, 40*(1), 1–7

Bloombaum, M., Yamamoto, J., & James, Q. (1968). Cultural stereotyping among psychotherapists. *Journal of Consulting and Clinical Psychology, 32*(1), 99.

Bryant-Davis, T., & Ocampo, C. (2007). A therapeutic approach to the treatment of racist-incident-based trauma. *Journal of Emotional Abuse, 6*(4), 1–22.

Carter, R. T. (2007). Racism and psychological and emotional injury: Recognizing and assessing race-based traumatic stress. *The Counseling Psychologist, 35*(1), 13–105.

Diemer, M. A., Kauffman, A., Koenig, N., Trahan, E., & Hsieh, C. A. (2006). Challenging racism, sexism, and social injustice: Support for urban adolescents' critical consciousness development. *Cultural Diversity and Ethnic Minority Psychology, 12*(3), 444.

Foster, R. P. (1999). An intersubjective approach to cross-cultural clinical work. *Smith College Studies in Social Work, 69*(2), 269–291.

Freud, S. (1910). *Future prospects of psychoanalytic therapy* (Vol. 11). Vintage Classics.

Godsil, R. D., & Richardson, L. S. (2017). Racial anxiety. *Iowa Law Review*, 102, 2235.

Green, J. W. (1982). *Cultural awareness in the human services*. Englewood Cliffs, NY: Prentice Hall.

Mosley, D. V., Hargons, C. N., Meiller, C., Angyal, B., Wheeler, P., Davis, C., & Stevens-Watkins, D. (2021). Critical consciousness of anti-Black racism: A practical model to prevent and resist racial trauma. *Journal of Counseling Psychology*, 68(1), 1.

Parke, R., & Clarke-Stewart, K. A. (2001, January). Effects of parental incarceration on young children. In *National policy conference. From prison to home: The effect of incarceration and reentry on children, families, and communities*.

Prilleltensky, I. (2003). Understanding, resisting, and overcoming oppression: Toward psychopolitical validity. *American Journal of Community Psychology, 31*(1–2), 195–201.

Prilleltensky, I. (2008). The role of power in wellness, oppression, and liberation: The promise of psychopolitical validity. *Journal of Community Psychology, 36*(2), 116–136.

Stampley, C. D. (2008). Social workers' culture-based countertransferences. *Journal of Ethnic & Cultural Diversity in Social Work, 17*(1), 37–59.

Williams, M. T., Metzger, I. W., Leins, C., & DeLapp, C. (2018). Assessing racial trauma within a DSM–5 framework: The UConn Racial/Ethnic Stress & Trauma Survey. *Practice Innovations, 3*(4), 242.

Chapter 10
Clinical Partnership: Application of Dismantling Anti-blackness Through Anti-oppressive Practice and Critical Consciousness

In this chapter, practitioners learn the most impactful practices to unpack their own biases and beliefs regarding those most impacted by the justice system. This supportive guide for clinical supervisors and trainers encourages the growth of awareness in complex systems of oppression impacting the trauma experienced by the child that are unique to their feelings and beliefs associated with parental incarceration. The overview of Critical Race Theory (CRT) and Culture-Based Countertransference (CBC) reinforces the clinician's ability to analyze, deconstruct, and transform power in the therapeutic session by using race as its point of engagement. CRT argues that white racism is a hegemonic socially and historically constructed cultural force in American society. Children impacted by parental incarceration commonly face stigma and shame associated with the criminalization of their parents; therefore, this chapter guides social workers in ways to use critical analytical tools to understand oppression and their own socialization within oppressive systems, as well as how this may show up in the therapeutic relationship both consciously and unconsciously. We develop a sense of agency and capacity to interrupt and change oppressive patterns and behaviors in ourselves and in the institutions and communities that we are part of. Insights gleaned from CBC can deepen social workers' awareness of relationship dynamics and provide valuable information about the therapeutic process. Case illustrations of how this practice is employed with children aged 8–16 years inform clinicians on specific tools they can use to make the therapeutic relationship feel safe and encouraging.

Despite the large number of children and families affected by incarceration, there has been very limited research conducted to explore the effects of parental incarceration on children and, in particular, the role that anti-racism has on treatment practice. While the literature finds that parental incarceration is associated with numerous negative effects in children, such as increased likelihood of future criminal justice system involvement (Huebner & Gustafson, 2007; Murray & Farrington, 2008; Roettger & Swisher, 2011); educational under-attainment, dropout, and grade

A. Morgan-Mullane, *An Integrative Approach to Clinical Social Work Practice with Children of Incarcerated Parents*, Essential Clinical Social Work Series,
https://doi.org/10.1007/978-3-031-28823-4_10

failure (Murray et al., 2012; Murray & Farrington, 2008; Phillips et al., 2006); and significant feelings of shame and stigmatization (Manning, 2011), limited research addresses the psychological impact of having a parent incarcerated. In addition, minimal research has been aimed at developing best practices, including educational and training requirements, for clinical social workers treating children and families affected by incarceration. Many children impacted by parental incarceration experience complex trauma through repetitive exposure to traumatizing events that are compounded by poverty and racism. Furthermore, children of incarcerated parents and their families represent an oppressed population—the vast majority of children of incarcerated parents and their families are members of minority groups—and thus experience racism in addition to a disproportionate percentage of arrests and incarcerations. Lastly, the loss of a parent or family member to incarceration adds additional levels of discrimination, often in the forms of stigmatizing behaviors derived from discriminatory stereotypes.

This chapter expands on the recognition that the phenomenon known as mass incarceration is associated with conscious and unconscious racial practices in social work that affect children of incarcerated parents. Contextual factors such as structural racism compound the impacts of mass incarceration on these children and have the potential to create inherent biases in clinicians and the general population alike. Clinicians will explore and recommend solutions to anti-Blackness in clinical practice, which refers to the unconscious racist beliefs and practices that fail to account for the historical and contextual needs and issues specific to populations affected by mass incarceration. This clinical overview provides clinicians with a comprehensive discussion around the historical oppression, specifically of the children of incarcerated parents, by defining anti-Blackness within the realm of social work from a micro, mezzo, and macro practice level to enhance therapeutic relationships for social workers treating children of incarcerated parents.

Establishing Parental Incarceration as a Primary Trauma

The United States leads the world in terms of incarceration with 2.2 million people currently in the nation's prisons and jails, representing a 500% increase over the last 40 years (Glaze & Maruschak, 2008). To underscore the extensive nature of this issue in US society, well over two million children have at least one incarcerated parent, according to the Bureau of Justice Statistics (Mumola, 2000), a number that is likely underreported because it does not consider the custodial states of individuals who are a child's guardian or who perform other significant caretaking functions (Manning, 2011; Miller et al., 2013; Murray & Farrington, 2008).

Children can exhibit the emotional effects of parental incarceration through complex trauma-related stress symptoms, such as isolation from their peers, anxiety, unhealthy interpersonal relationships, concentration problems, sleep difficulties, emotional withdrawal from family members, substance use or dependence, and significant feelings of shame and secrecy. If unaddressed, the impacts of these symptoms can often lead to long-term psychological and emotional malfunctioning (Manning, 2011; Miller & Barnes, 2015; Murray et al., 2012; Phillips et al., 2006). According to the US Department of Justice (Mumola, 2000), without intervention, 70% of these children will follow in the footsteps of their parent(s) and enter the juvenile and/or adult criminal justice system. Parental incarceration also threatens the future liberty of the children themselves by placing them at a far greater risk of future criminal justice involvement.

Arditti's (2005) ecological approach to incarceration aimed to holistically understand the effects of incarceration on the interrelationships between family members, environments, and society and asserts that incarceration may produce multiplicative harms on children and families. These interconnected harms—strained parent-child relationships, difficulties associated with traveling to and visiting custodial settings, community reactions to re-entry, and stigma—have the potential to be linked with and reinforce one another. Because they experience intersectional sources of trauma, children of incarcerated parents are a highly vulnerable population. However, due to stigmatization and secrecy, children of incarcerated parents are broadly viewed as an "invisible population" (Phillips & Gates, 2011).

Parental incarceration itself can be seen as a symptom of existing trauma and/or a direct cause of trauma-symptom development. The overlapping racial, social, and structural disadvantages experienced by the majority of children of incarcerated parents will make it difficult to isolate the causal effects of parental incarceration on the development of trauma symptoms; even without this information, parental incarceration is a strong predictor of child trauma. Many children affected by parental incarceration experience complex traumas made manifest by sustained and repeated traumatic experiences such as racism, poverty, diminished social mobility, lack of access to resources, and low employability that are increasingly common for poor minority children (Wildeman & Western, 2010) and are found to be associated with trauma development (National Research Council, 2014). Even prior to their parent's incarceration, these children experience an elevated risk for trauma-symptom development and social marginalization (Wildeman & Western, 2010).

The number of children with parents in prison has increased 80% between 1991 and 2007 (Glaze & Maruschak, 2008). Nationally, approximately 20% of children with an incarcerated parent in state prison are younger than 4 years old, approximately 60% are between 5 and 14 years of age, and approximately 16% are 15–17 years old (Turanovic et al., 2012). One-third of all children will be at least 18 years old by the time their incarcerated parent is released from prison. For most caretakers, parental incarceration is a negative event; it can produce financial insecurity, elevate emotional stress, strain interpersonal relationships, and increase difficulties associated with the supervision of children (Turanovic et al., 2012).

Children of incarcerated parents experience numerous sources of material and emotional insecurity. For example, children of incarcerated parents are more likely to receive public assistance, to experience interrupted phone or utility service due to non-payment, and to experience residential insecurity through missed mortgage and rental payments (Geller et al., 2009). These examples are symptoms of the greater socioeconomic disadvantage that exists for these children even before a parent is incarcerated, and these conditions tend to worsen after incarceration (Miller & Barnes, 2015; Phillips et al., 2006). Besides material consequences, a parent's incarceration can abruptly dismantle a family. Children of incarcerated parents are less likely to live in a home with both parents present (Geller et al., 2009) and are sometimes placed indefinitely in foster care while family members are sent to distant penitentiaries, making travel and visitation difficult for families with limited resources and few transportation options (Manning, 2011).

Parental incarceration also threatens the future liberty of children by placing them at a far greater risk of future criminal justice involvement. Using data from Add Health, a national panel dataset that includes 20,700 respondents in grades 7–12, Roettger and Swisher (2011) determined that parental incarceration is highly and significantly correlated with increased likelihood of arrest before age 25. Huebner and Gustafson (2007) found that parental incarceration nearly triples a child's risk of future criminal justice involvement and that children of incarcerated parents are up to three times more likely to be incarcerated than counterparts who did not experience parental incarceration. A meta-analysis conducted by Murray and Farrington (2008) confirmed these findings and further concluded that these effects were exacerbated when the child was without additional protective factors such as supportive communities, therapeutic outlets, or friends and family to whom they can talk, or if they reside within especially punitive environments. There are significant racial disparities as well: In a sample of children who experienced parental incarceration, Black and Hispanic children were, respectively, 39.2% and 46.7% more likely than white children to be arrested before they reached age 25 (Roettger & Swisher, 2011).

Parental incarceration also poses an emotional risk to children. As early as age three, children of incarcerated parents can begin to exhibit signs of emotional distress like anger, aggression, and difficulty attaching to primary caregivers (Geller et al., 2009). Well into adolescence and young adulthood, the emotional effects of parental incarceration can be exhibited in the forms of depression, anxiety, inability to build relationships, concentration problems, sleep difficulties, emotional withdrawal, substance use or dependence, and significant feelings of shame and stigmatization (Manning, 2011; Miller & Barnes, 2015; Murray et al., 2012; Phillips et al., 2006), all of which are trauma-related stress symptoms. These emotional and behavioral symptoms have far-reaching consequences and may partially explain educational under-attainment and school-based difficulties, such as truancy, dropout, and grade failure, that are more common among children of incarcerated parents (Murray et al., 2012; Murray & Farrington, 2008; Phillips et al., 2006).

Growing research on the number of children and adolescents impacted by the loss of a parent to incarceration requires that social workers and other mental health practitioners consider the unique clinical needs of this population and employ therapeutic best practices. Because African American and other ethnic minority youth are more likely to be affected by parental incarceration (Foster & Hagan, 2013), the specific clinical practices require practitioners to utilize anti-oppressive interventions that incorporate a full comprehension of past and present implications of mass incarceration. Only in this way are we able to combat conscious and unconscious discriminatory behaviors and beliefs that exist within the social work profession and that consequently reinforce anti-Blackness.

Racial Policing That Targets Families of Color

Research addressing mass incarceration has reported a rising and disproportionate number of African American men and women who have been arrested and incarcerated. In 2008, the Pew Center on the States reported that Black men are incarcerated at a rate that is nearly seven times the rate of white men of similar ages: 1 in every 15 Black males aged 18 and over had been incarcerated, compared to 1 in every 106 white males. Using data from the US Department of Justice, Nellis (2015) found that African Americans were incarcerated in state prisons at 5.1 times the rate of imprisonment for whites. The author explained this disparity as related to harsh sentences for drug-related crime, implicit judicial bias, and structural disadvantages affecting African Americans before they enter the criminal justice system. Enos (2017) found that race and ethnicity are often determinants of the frequency at which men and women are likely to be stopped for traffic violations, arrested following a police stop, or victims of police violence.

This increase in the rates of men and women of color who are under correctional supervision has a direct effect on the number of children who grow up in homes where a parent is absent because they are under custodial supervision, a fact that is often underreported. As of 2016, five million children in the United States had one or both parents incarcerated at some point before they reached 18 years of age (Annie E. Casey Foundation, 2016). These higher rates of arrest are likely associated with the greater frequency of police contact experienced by people of color. Much research has indicated that people of color are more likely to be subjected to police "stop-and-frisks" that frequently lead to an arrest (Goel et al., 2016). Goel et al. (2016) explained that the disparity in stop-and-frisk rates is partially attributable to less stringent policing practices that result in circumstances where police demonstrate a "lower threshold for stopping minorities relative to similarly situated whites" (p. 365). The authors also found that stop-and-frisk disparities were partially the result of a decision to increase these activities within high-crime areas, particularly in public housing, both of which constitute predominantly minority neighborhoods. As a result of policing practices that target specific neighborhoods, there are also drastic differences in rates of arrest. For example, in the predominantly white Park Slope neighborhood of New York City, there were a total of 63 marijuana arrests in 2016; in the adjacent Crown Heights neighborhood, which has a much larger minority population, there were 362 arrests over the same period (Cheney, 2017).

Mass incarceration has been defined as a rigid system of laws, policies, and institutions that collectively ensure the inferior status of a group defined specifically by race (Alexander, 2012). Individuals of color, who are more likely to be incarcerated than white individuals, face substantial barriers to stability because of a previous arrest. Many lose the ability to obtain federal benefits, such as student loans to support higher education; they lose access to public housing, thus placing their residential stability at risk; they face barriers to employment based on social stigma; and many forfeit their right to vote, thus making it even less possible for them to elect representatives to serve their interests (Legal Action Center, 2004). Given that mass incarceration unevenly affects people of color, these barriers to re-entry are more likely to disenfranchise large swaths of Black individuals from participation in the so-called mainstream society. In *The New Jim Crow*, Alexander (2012) defined mass incarceration as a system that "locks people not only behind actual bars in actual prisons, but also behind virtual bars and virtual walls—walls that are invisible to the naked eye but function nearly as effectively as Jim Crow Laws once did" (p. 12). Alexander was referring to a criminal justice system that unfairly persecutes Black individuals and then strips them of their rights even after serving a period of incarceration, effectively making these individuals permanently imprisoned.

This drastic increase in the prison population over the last 40 years hardly sheds light on the depths of the profound loss experienced by these many Black men and women, their communities, schools, homes, and children. It is often the case that mass incarceration is viewed specifically by the numbers, with alarming statistics gaining more prominence in recent years. However, even as awareness of these startling statistics grows, less attention is paid to the so-called "collateral consequences" of incarceration, which can deeply and profoundly affect the children and family members who are left behind. Social workers who strive to actively address historical and current systems of oppression must embrace this knowledge of acute traumatic loss. Social workers need to be educated about not only the vastly growing numbers of those impacted by the criminal justice system, but also the unique needs of their children and families, who are often the silent victims of mass incarceration. Parental incarceration is a traumatic event for a child because they suffer from mental health problems at least twice as much compared to children without incarcerated parents (Hoffman, 2017). A social worker's full comprehension of the historical, social, and familial implications of mass incarceration is critical to the effective employment of fully comprehensive anti-oppressive interventions; without such knowledge, clinicians risk perpetuating anti-Blackness values within communities of color.

The Cultural Challenge of Cultural Competence

Social work practice that does not accommodate the diverse cultural needs and backgrounds of service users is somewhat common. A study by Parrott (2009) exemplified how people from ethnic minority communities continue to feel as though service providers are responding inappropriately to their needs as they utilize a lens of "mono-cultural" practice that does not address the vastness of languages, religions, and cultures shared throughout many minority communities.

Cultural competence, generally described as the awareness, knowledge, and skills essential for social workers to develop within their own practice to advance culturally appropriate services to clients within the working relationship (Danso, 2017), encourages social workers to develop knowledge for supporting culturally marginalized populations to address the exploitative use of power. This knowledge acquisition is often reduced to in-class curricula, with social work students only receiving specific information about affected populations, if any related information at all. Often, many common social work populations, including justice-involved individuals, are not discussed in detail within social work curricula. Despite the high prevalence of justice-involved clients in our profession, only 5% of all Master of Social Work programs in the United States provide a concentration in criminal justice and only 22% offer a criminal justice course (Epperson et al., 2013). Currently, despite a robust emphasis on clinicians' cultural awareness, we have not established social work education and curricula that adequately prepare social work students to immediately understand the populations with which we work. To do so requires not only modifications to our curricula, but also a change in our pedagogy that enables social workers to go beyond the awareness of social justice principles, which will help social workers to address the differences in their own competence from the populations they serve and allow them to form a better working alliance with these individuals.

Social workers have also been reluctant to acknowledge the power differentials created within their working relationships. By failing to reduce the hierarchical dynamic established when the social worker adopts the "expert" role in his or her therapeutic relationship, the therapy proceeds without recognizing the client as the expert in their own life. Therefore, social workers must be encouraged and guided to have discussions about oppressive experiences, and this education removes the conscious and unconscious relationship of "teacher/student" and reconstructs the therapeutic relationship as a partnership (Sakamoto & Pitner, 2005). The inclusion of anti-oppressive practice will proliferate empowerment values that are often absent from research on social work practices (Danso, 2017).

In social work, academic settings curricula can intentionally or unintentionally "socialize social work students to adhere to the interests in the dominant groups, reinforcing class and racial ideology, despite overt promotion of social justice and diversity principles" (Bhuyan et al., 2017, p. 375). Rosen et al. (2017) provided more clear examples of the pedagogical limitations of social work education:

> Though these pedagogical efforts have been implemented to promote cultural self-awareness, diversity courses in schools of social work have not historically followed an intersectional approach when providing information and content on the range of groups with whom social workers are practicing. That is, content from courses had often centered on skills needed for working with specific marginalized groups and had been delivered unidimensionally across the course of the school term. For example, one class session would focus on working with African Americans, another on working with women, another with working with LGBTQ populations, and so on. However, such an approach is problematic for several reasons. Most importantly, this approach is problematic because each of these groups contains an incredible amount of diversity within it, and there is no formula for working with its members. (p. 290-291)

For social workers to avoid complicit engagement in practices that reinforce power dynamics, they must draw on the social, emotional, and physical expertise of the client. Rather than reducing their knowledge of an individual to some generalized conception of the group, anti-oppressive practice encourages the social worker to recognize the unique differences of each individual they work with, regardless of the group. The group to which they belong may provide valuable historical context to the individual context, but it should not dominate one's thinking about the individual's treatment. Historical context of culture and community must be used as guides in the service process. Otherwise, social workers will be unable to offer partnership to communities such as those impacted by mass incarceration and, specifically, parental incarceration without acknowledging the intergenerational trauma of colonialism, racism, slavery, and other forms of cultural devastation.

Present Applications of Anti-oppressive Practice in Clinical Practice

The term *anti-oppressive practice* (AOP) tends to describe a combination of anti-discriminatory and anti-oppressive practices that draw on both Marxist and feminist ideologies (Sakamoto & Pitner, 2005). According to Sakamoto and Pitner, AOP aims for the "eradication of oppression through institutional and societal changes" (p. 436). Pollack (2004) describes AOP as a framework that draws upon a variety of approaches such as "feminist, critical, anti-racist, post-structural, and postmodern theories of practice" (p. 693). This framework aims to de-individualize clients' problems to understand them within the wider social context of their lives (Pollack, 2004). AOP is an important guiding framework for clinicians working with clients who have been affected by mass incarceration. It encourages the clinician to take a more active role in understanding the institutional and societal effects on their clients and to enact changes in those realms. Whereas clinical social work is traditionally thought to be a micro-level practice where the emphasis is on the therapeutic relationship, AOP encourages social workers to consider the critical interaction between the institutional effects of mass incarceration on the clinical dimension. Given this relationship, social workers cannot isolate their focus on the clinical dimension alone; they must also consider the effects of institutions, systems, and society on the clients they serve.

Utilizing AOP can be challenging for some on the clinical level as it does not always account for the navigation of this complex terrain to ensure that dominant beliefs and values are not guiding the intervention in session only to reinforce oppressive practices. The intended result is that treatment is guided by the client's own experiences with dominant or oppressive structures, rather than by the social worker's experience as the de facto expert in the roles and issues thought to be pertinent for each client. This inclusive practice of making the client the expert in their own life promises a safe and transformative experience for both the client and the social worker. The problematic behaviors exhibited by the client then become less individually pathologized and can be viewed by both the social worker and client as appropriate responses to systems of oppression and intergenerational and historical trauma. Social workers then reconceptualize racism, sexual violence, homophobia, poverty, etc., when addressing the mental health needs of those they serve within a wider social context (Pollack, 2005).

AOP embodies a person-centered philosophy and values system concerned with reducing the damaging effects of structural inequalities in people's lives, and the practice focuses on both process and outcome as a way of measuring the relationship between the social worker and client (Strier & Binyamin, 2012). This practice occurs by developing a non-hierarchical therapeutic alliance between the social worker and client. The client is meant to feel safe and understood by the social worker through an AOP lens. These practices reinforce the requirement that social workers put forth all necessary effort to change the composition of a therapeutic intervention and overall service delivery through macro changes in policies and organizational transformations (Sakamoto & Pitner, 2005).

However, the lofty promises of this model to adequately address all social justice issues present the greatest challenge for social workers. There is very little literature on how to effectively apply these principles in a clinical context, given that most social workers already believe that they are practicing through an anti-oppressive lens. Nevertheless, if significant historical information is missing from social workers' comprehension of the person with whom they are working, there is potential for the power dynamic to remain in place whereby the social worker perpetually reinforces power differentials and social injustice (Sakamoto & Pitner, 2005).

Critical Consciousness Framework in Clinical Practice

Without a vital chronological framework and acknowledgment of profound historical trauma on a social, emotional, and cellular level of the human body and spirit, social workers will be unable to access the insight needed to take action effectively and responsibly. The critical consciousness framework is a clinical social work practice that encourages social workers to be introspective about the power and privilege they embody and specifically how this power and privilege is experienced in the therapeutic relationship (O'Neill, 2015). According to O'Neill:

> Such active critical awareness and power differentials is purposeful in the social worker's efforts to support the power of those served. To that end, critical consciousness requires intentional and ongoing self-reflection that addresses one's perception of self and others, social location and identities, relational intersections, forces of oppression with the environment, bias, assumptions, and the dynamics of power and privilege. (p. 628)

Inherent bias in social work practice creates conditions that are the inverse of the conditions explained by O'Neill (2015) in the critical consciousness framework. Critical consciousness encourages self-awareness, knowledge development, and a deeper understanding of the client's historical and social contexts to encourage the social worker to recognize their power in the clinical practice and how that power affects the decision-making process. In this way, the therapeutic relationship becomes less about a clinician imposing a certain treatment on a client and more about the client and clinician co-creating an appropriate treatment based on the client's expressed needs, with the clinician supporting this type of exploration. A critical consciousness framework forces a social worker to continually confront the implications of his or her own power and the differentials created by them. Through the utilization of a critical consciousness framework, social workers become actively accountable for the legacy of anti-Blackness practices in clinical interventions and social work practice.

Anti-blackness Defined

Anti-oppressive practice is a generalized term that is meant to encompass a response to a variety of oppressive practices (e.g., racism, sexism, anti-queer bias). In many ways—regardless of the diffuse nature of various oppressive experiences—AOP can elicit an overly broad response to any problematic behavior instead of creating a fixed and precise target. Therefore, it is important to recognize that an anti-oppressive lens, in and of itself, has the potential to dilute and be reductive, minimizing the targeted need and the specificity of the response. In a report to the Ontario Premier, former Canadian Democratic Leader and United Nations Special Envoy for HIV/AIDS in Africa Steven Lewis described why anti-Black racism requires description that is different and more pronounced:

> While it is obviously true that every visible minority community experiences indignities and wounds of systemic discrimination...it is the Black community which is the focus. It is Blacks who are being shot, it is Black youth that is unemployed in excessive numbers, it is Black students who are being inappropriately streamed in schools, it is Black kids who are disproportionately dropping out, it is housing communities with large concentrations of Black residents where the sense of vulnerability and disadvantage is most acute, it is Black employees, professional and non-professional, on whom the doors of upward equity slam shut. Just as the soothing balm of 'multiculturalism' cannot mask racism, so racism cannot mask its primary target. (Lewis, 1992)

Douglas (2017) and Woods (2013) provided an extensive overview of how anti-Blackness is rooted in ancient Greek and Roman scholarly writing that identifies color prejudice as an integral consideration in their thinking and culture (Douglas, 2017). During the fifteenth and sixteenth centuries, historians have concluded, the narrative of anti-Blackness became most noticeable during the earliest infiltrations into the African continent (Douglas, 2017). The descriptions of Africans as "Black" became the defining description of "subspecies of humanity" (Woods, 2013, p. 126). This was because the human race had originally been seen as normatively white from a Western perspective and introducing the color of Blackness as "other" racialized human beings. Therefore, the beginning of an attitude and moral belief of anti-Blackness then provided the appealing rationalization for enslavement and other brutal acts of violence against the bodies of Black men and women (Douglas, 2017). The relationship this historical context has to present-day mass incarceration, slavery, and racism is the continuum of oppression and dehumanization of the masses of people suffering in communities that are structured in dominance (Sexton, 2010). This current recognition of the anti-Black narrative not only includes the discussion of colonization in both Africa and America, but it is also woven throughout the exploitation of labor in the prison systems, the subordination of minority cultures through current forms of gentrification, and the overall extermination of basic human rights as portrayed through policies and laws that prohibit formerly incarcerated men and women to participate in equal education and employment opportunities, voting rights, and access to housing.

Addressing Anti-blackness in Anti-oppressive Clinical Practice

To unequivocally address anti-Blackness in social work, practitioners have a responsibility to educate and aid other social workers as well as social work students in an effective self-reflective process which names their own complacency and place within systems of systemic racism and oppression. According to Trevalon and Murray-Garcia (1998), *cultural humility* refers to a process whereby a clinician critiques his or her own biases in an effort to rectify the power imbalances that exist within the therapeutic relationship. Foronda et al. (2016) further define cultural humility as a continuous, lifelong process. Through this introspective, self-exploratory process, a clinician questions and challenges the implicit assumptions that they have developed toward a group and considers how this existing thinking might uphold unhelpful power dynamics. Critical cultural humility in micro anti-oppressive practice will address social work's alignment with dominant social and political ideologies that have intertwined the profession in oppressive practices, exemplified in social work's participation in the cultural genocide of communities of color, and continued in their overrepresentation in child welfare services. This continual subjugation and marginalization exemplify the failure to speak to systemic inequality in social work practice (Bhuyan et al., 2017).

Oppression is often a covert and difficult phenomenon to recognize. For individuals affected by systemic racism, many symptoms of the oppressive structures may mask a clinician's ability to recognize the underlying systems of oppression that affect the client. For example, systemic racism has resulted in millions of African Americans experiencing poverty, mental illness, residential instability, and incarceration; these symptoms of oppression are very noticeable and may be treated first, without addressing the underlying social structure and the implications of the social structure on that client. Social work today requires a greater understanding of the intersectionality of racism, poverty, justice-system involvement, and mental illness—all are factors that interact with one another and contribute to the phenomenon we describe as mass incarceration.

Historical and present-day contexts of slavery, mass incarceration, oppression, and ongoing discriminatory challenges are all critical components required to develop a micro anti-oppressive practice. In line with anti-oppressive practice, contemporary social workers must seek to dismantle anti-Blackness, which is defined as the systemic forms of oppression that exist against African Americans at a societal level (e.g., mass incarceration, limited economic mobility, discriminatory hiring practices, overly punitive disciplinary practices in schools). Understanding the existence of these discriminatory practices as anti-Black is critical to honoring the legacy of colonialism, slavery, and capitalism on African Americans. The continual mistreatment of African Americans lends credence to the idea that AOP should be further refined to specifically denote practices that attempt to dismantle anti-Blackness. Cross-cultural research and clinical interventions in social work should aim to disassemble a legacy of anti-Blackness practices in social services. Trauma-informed trainings; curricula that include coursework on mass incarceration, justice involvement, and the collateral consequences of arrest and incarceration; clinical supervision based in principles of cultural humility; and personal self-awareness grounded in critical consciousness all ensure that social workers can overcome the limitations that have existed in social work education and practice.

Therefore, the need to strengthen and include a clear overview of anti-Blackness history is necessary in social work education, clinical applications of culturally appropriate interventions for practitioners, and clinical supervision for new and veteran social workers. Because existing social work curricula can be inadequate in their descriptions of the role that mass incarceration and systematic racism have played in the lives of individuals who are subjugated by it, many practicing clinicians have limited academic exposure to these concepts and conditions. Where such matters are discussed and taught in the classroom—or even in the case of a veteran social worker who is familiar with these oppressive structures via frequent contact with an exposed population—the end result is not that the social worker then possesses an unparalleled level of expertise and thus fully comprehends the dynamic. The nature of the anti-oppressive clinical practice is that clients act as co-equals in treatment and social workers defer to the client to explain the circumstances of oppressive social factors. Thus, the experience of children, adolescents, men, and women who have suffered from systems of oppression developed throughout the mass incarceration era should be considered valuable information for clinical treatment and the clients themselves should be viewed as "co-leaders" in an anti-oppressive clinical treatment (Danso, 2017).

While past practice generally positions the social worker in a role of professional authority, AOP requires the clinician to recognize their own lack of exposure to the direct oppressive circumstances the client has experienced. As a co-equal in the therapeutic treatment dynamic, the client can draw upon personal experiences of oppression to form knowledge that can inform the rest of the treatment. Failing to recognize the difference between practical and personal experience can be a significant misstep in anti-oppressive practice because it reinforces a hierarchical dynamic and bolsters a cycle of dominance and oppression by placing the therapist in a superior position that does not require them to acknowledge their own racial or cultural biases. Poor relationships or alliances with the clients who do not feel safe and valued as equal partners in treatment and the social worker are commonly associated with children dropping out of treatment prematurely (Turanovic & Rodriguez, 2017).

Employing Cultural Humility and Critical Consciousness with Children of Incarcerated Parents

Social justice practices have remained separate or distinct from micro or clinical practices (Bhuyan et al., 2017). The lack of integration of social justice principles within social work education underlines the "whiteness" (Bhuyan et al., 2017) and dominant perspective currently facing clinical social work practice. For this reason, the social work profession must seek instructors who teach and clinically supervise through a lens of self-reflection and can comfortably address their own working relationship to historically oppressive practices. These educators, supervisors, advocates, and trainers must challenge the structures and procedures of all service delivery to families impacted by incarceration. Only by using the framework of how intergenerational trauma impacts psychological, biological, and community functioning stemming back to Africa in the sixteenth and seventeenth centuries can the effectiveness of these narratives teach and clearly inform social work practice on how anti-Blackness results in the denigration and dehumanization of Black people (Douglas, 2017).

Parental incarceration is considered an adverse childhood experience, a designation which, coupled with additional risk factors, has been shown to be predictive of trauma development (Afifi et al., 2011; Arditti & Savla, 2015). Many, if not all, children affected by parental incarceration experience depression, functional and cognitive impairments, anxiety, and disruptive, antisocial, and externalizing behaviors that are each symptoms of trauma. These risk factors are compounded by a variety of other racial, structural, and environmental risk factors that are correlated with parental incarceration, which, in and of themselves, expose children to risk for trauma-related symptomatology.

Cultural adaptations to clinical interventions, training in community- and school-based settings, and the inclusion of necessary curricula in graduate-level social programs are all required to effectually dismantle anti-Blackness and other oppressive practices with children of incarcerated parents. It is essential that social workers appropriately identify the collateral consequences of parental incarceration while addressing the unique needs of this population in direct practice. Turney (2017) emphasizes that trauma-informed care oriented to the concepts of ambiguous loss, stigma, and shame must be considered to achieve best clinical practices and interventions for children of incarcerated parents.

Children of incarcerated parents are undoubtedly a high-risk population for trauma-related symptom development, and this necessitates the exploration and utilization of effective interventions and treatments that can be adequately applied to this population. Therefore, adaptations to effective individual clinical interventions, such as trauma-focused cognitive behavioral therapy, narrative therapy, and attachment therapy, offer clients the opportunity to embrace the personal narrative of their historical and present trauma, as well as maintain the expert and educator roles in their own life. The trauma experienced by most individuals is multi-faceted, incorporating their own or a family member's experience with the justice system, while also being compounded by societal conditions such as poverty, racism, and stigma that have further harmed them. The utilization of trauma-informed care, narrative therapy, and attachment therapy is in recognition of the multiplicative and cumulative traumas that have been experienced but are marginalized by social workers, as a result of either conscious or unconscious anti-Blackness. Children with incarcerated parents are more likely than their counterparts to be placed in special education programs and be held back in elementary school (Turney, 2017). Therefore, with more school absences and declining high school performance, school social workers must be vigilant about acknowledging the particular academic needs and services for this population to maintain awareness of the historical and present construction of the school-to-prison pipeline that greatly impacts mass incarceration.

The critical dismantling of anti-Blackness in the social work field is needed for effective understanding of the psychological manifestations of trauma symptoms related to parental incarceration. The foundation begins in our MSW institutions, education, and clinical supervision for the new social worker as well as the seasoned practitioner. Presently in clinical practice, there is a substantial percentage of experienced social workers who employ language that still does not embody or evidence an awareness of social justice issues (Irizarry et al., 2016).

Clinical anti-oppressive practices will aid in breaking the cycle of intergenerational incarceration by enabling social workers to utilize essential cultural adaptations in working with the individual child, the family, and the community (Luther, 2015) impacted by incarceration. By bridging the gap in social work research and social justice values in clinical practice, social workers will avoid contributing to ineffective or poorer quality of services and deepening the marginalization of oppressed communities (Danso, 2017), such as children of incarcerated parents, the silent victims of mass incarceration.

Reflection Questions

1. Define the term "Anti-Blackness."
2. Explore the use of Critical Race Theory in clinical practice, and was this theory one you learned in your clinical classes?
3. How do we as a profession reinforce the urgency around dismantling racial harms within our clinical community?
4. How might the harms you've identified most impact clinical work with children suffering from the loss of a parent to the carceral system?

References

Afifi, T., Mather, A., Boman, J., Fleisher, W., Enns, M., MacMillan, H., & Sareen, J. (2011) Childhood adversity and personality disorders: Results from a nationally representative population-based study. *Journal of Psychiatric Research,* pp. 814–822.

Alexander, M. (2012). *The new Jim crow: Mass incarceration in the age of colorblindness.* The New Press.

Annie, E. (2016). *Casey foundation.*

Arditti, J. A. (2005). Families and incarceration: An ecological approach. *Families in Society, 86*(2), 251–260.

Arditti, J., & Savla, J. (2015) Parental incarceration and child trauma symptoms in single caregiver homes. *Journal of Child and Family Studies, 24*(3), 551–561.

Bhuyan, R., Bejan, R., & Jayapal, D.. (2017) Social workers' perspectives on social justice in social work education: When mainstreaming social justice masks structural inequalities. *Social Work Education, 36*(4), 373–390.

Cheney, B. (2017, February 6) Marijuana arrests in city increased in 2016, with large racial disparities. *Politico.* Received from https://www.politico.com

Danso, R. (2017). An integrated framework of critical cultural competence and anti-oppressive practice for social justice social work research. *Qualitative Social Work, 14*(4), 572–588.

Douglas, B. K. (2017). Stop the violence: Breaking the cycle of anti-black violence. *A Journal of Bible and Theology, 71*(4), 398–407.

Enos, S. (2017). Another war on women: Mass incarceration, Gender and Color. *International Review of Modern Sociology, 43*(1), 34–56.

Epperson, M., Roberts, L., Ivanoff, A., Tripodi, S., & Gilmer, C. (2013). To what extent is criminal justice content specifically addressed in MSW programs? *Journal of Social Work Education, 49*(1), 96–107.

Foronda, C., Baptiste, D., Reinholdt, M., & Ousman, K. (2016). Cultural humility: A concept analysis. *Journal of Transcultural Nursing, 27*, 210–217.

Foster, H., & Hagan, J. (2013). Maternal and paternal imprisonment in the stress process. *Social Science Research, 42*, 650–669.

Geller, A., Garfinkel, I., Cooper, C. E., & Mincy, R. B. (2009) Parental incarceration and child well-being: Implications for urban families. *Social Science Quarterly, 90*(5), 1186–1202.

Glaze, L., & Maruschak, L. (2008). *Parents in prison and their minor children.* Bureau of Justice Statistics.

Goel, S., Rao, J. M., & Shroff, R. (2016). Precinct or prejudice? Understanding racial disparities in New York City's stop-and-frisk policy. *The Annals of Applied Statistics 10*(1), 365–394.

Hoffman, A. A. (2017). Mass Incarceration's second generation-the unintended victims of the Carceral State and thinking about alternatives to punishment through restorative justice. *Race and Social Justice Law Review, 7*, 247–274.

Huebner, B. M., & Gustafson, R. (2007). The effect of maternal incarceration on adult offspring in the criminal justice system. *Journal of Criminal Justice, 35*(3), 283–296.

Irizarry, C., Marlowe, M. J., Hallahan, L., & Bull, M. (2016). Restoring connections: Social workers' practice wisdom towards achieving social justice. *British Journal of Social Work, 46*, 1855–1871.

Legal Action Center. (2004). *After Prison: Roadblocks to Reentry.* Retrieved from Lewis, 1992.http://lac.org/roadblocks-to-reentry/upload/lacreport/LAC_PrintReport.pdf

Lewis, J. (1992). Gender and the development of welfare regimes. *Journal of European Social Policy, 2*(3), 159–173.

Luther, K. (2015). Examining social support among adult children of incarcerated parents. *Interdisciplinary Journal of Applied Family Studies, 64*, 505–518.

Manning, R. (2011) Punishing the innocent: Children of incarcerated and detained parents. *Criminal Justice Ethics, 30*(3), 267–287.

Miller, H. V., & Barnes, J. C. (2015). The association between parental incarceration and health, education, and economic outcomes in young adulthood. *American Journal of Criminal Justice, 40*, 765–784.

Miller, A. L., Perryman, J., Markovitz, L., Franzen, S., Cochran, S., & Brown, S. (2013). Strengthening incarcerated families: Evaluating a pilot program for children of incarcerated parents and their caregivers. *Family Relations, 62*, 584–596.

Mumola, C. J. (2000). *Incarcerated parents and their children.* U.S. Department of Justice, Office of Justice Programs, Bureau of Justice Statistics.

Murray, J., & Farrington, D. P. (2008). The effects of parental imprisonment on children. *Crime and Justice, 37*(1), 133–206.

Murray, J., Farrington, D. P., & Sekol, I. (2012) Children's antisocial behavior, mental health, drug use, and educational performance after parental incarceration: A systematic review and meta-analysis. *Psychological Bulletin, 138*(2), 175–210.

National Research Council. (2014). *New directions in child abuse and neglect research.*

Nellis, A. (2015). *A return to justice: Rethinking our approach to juveniles in the system.* Rowman & Littlefield.

O'Neill, M. (2015). Applying critical consciousness and evidence-based practice decision-making: A framework for clinical social work practice. *Journal of Social Work Education, 51*(4), 624–637.

Parrott, L. (2009). Constructive marginality: Conflicts and dilemmas in cultural competence and anti-oppressive practice. *Social Work Education, 28*(6), 617–630.

Phillips, S. D., & Gates, T. (2011) A conceptual framework for understanding the stigmatization of children of incarcerated parents. *Journal of Child and Family Studies, 20*, 286–294.

Phillips, S. D., Erkanki, A., Keeler, G. P., Costello, E. J., & Angold, A. (2006) Disentangling the risks: Parents criminal justice involvement and Children's exposure to family risks. *Criminology & Public Policy, 5*(4): 677–702.

Pollack, S. (2004). Anti-oppressive social work practice with women in prison: Discursive reconstructions and alternative practices. *British Journal of Social Work, 34*, 693–707.

Pollack, S. (2005). Taming the shrew: Regulating prisoners through women-centered mental health programming. *Critical Criminology, 13*(1), 71–87.

Roettger, M. E., & Swisher, R. R. (2011) Associations of fathers' history of incarceration with sons' delinquency and arrest among black, white, and Hispanic males in the United States. *Criminology, 49*(4), 1109–1147.

Rosen, D., McCall, J., & Goodkind, S. (2017). Teaching critical self-reflection through the lens of cultural humility: An assignment in a social work diversity course. *Social Work Education, 36*(3), 289–298.

Sakamoto, I., & Pitner, R. O. (2005). Use of critical consciousness in anti-oppressive social work practice: Disentangling power dynamics at personal and structural levels. *The British Journal of Social Work, 35*(4), 435–452.

Sexton, J. (2010). "The curtain of the sky": An introduction. *Critical Sociology, 36*(1), 11–24.

Strier, R., & Binyamin, S.. (2012) Introducing anti-oppressive social work practice in public services: Rhetoric to practice. *British Journal of Social Work, 44*, 2095–2112.

Trevalon, M., & Murray-Garcia, J. (1998). Cultural humility versus cultural competence: A critical distinction in defining training outcomes in multicultural education. *Journal of Health Care for the Poor and Underserved, 9*, 117–125.

Turanovic, J. J., & Rodriguez, N. (2017). Mental health service needs in the prison boom: The case of children of incarcerated mothers. *Criminal Justice Policy Review, 28*(5), 415–436.

Turanovic, J. J., Rodriguez, N., & Pratt, T. C. (2012). The collateral consequences of incarceration revisited: A qualitative analysis of the effects on caregivers of children of incarcerated parents. *Criminology, 50*(4), 913–959.

Turney, K. (2017). The unequal consequences of mass incarceration for children. *Demography, 54*, 361–389.

Wildeman, C., & Western, B. (2010). Incarceration in fragile families. *The Future of Children, 20*, 157–177.

Woods, P. T. (2013). Surrogate selves: Notes on anti-trafficking and anti-blackness. *Social Identities, 19*(1), 120–134.

Chapter 11
An Integrative Model to Transform Clinical Practice

Children of Promise, NYC: An Anti-racist Clinical Healing Community for Children of Incarcerated Parents

Children of Promise, NYC (CPNYC) is a community-based mental health approach to treating intergenerational trauma experienced by children of incarcerated parents. Within this setting, established and founded by Sharon Content, the programming design is centered on the explicit narratives of injustice, racial trauma, and need for community healing identified uniquely by the children in the organization and their family members. Collective access to liberation and healing is woven throughout the framework of clinical care, training, and supervision for all mental healthcare providers serving this community. The application of anti-racist therapeutic models, mitigation practices, policy, and advocacy reinforces the active commitment to dismantling anti-Blackness practices in mental healthcare experienced by children of incarcerated parents. The autonomy and dignity of every child within the organization speaks to the liberation each seeks from the numerous carceral systems that have directly victimized and brutalized both themselves and their parents.

Children of Promise, NYC seeks to be an institution that actively works toward equity in service provision, offers access to resources beyond therapeutic care, and delivers a program design that addresses the comprehensive needs of children and their imprisoned parents. The program model aims to guide collective community healing that moves beyond individual survival and seeks revolutionary change through the voice and power of children of incarcerated parents. CPNYC's mentoring, re-entry, adult and child therapeutic, and academic programming identifies the urgency in wraparound services for communities impacted by the injustice system and the pervasive structural traumas that continue to exist as a result of racial violence perpetuated by mass incarceration.

A. Morgan-Mullane, *An Integrative Approach to Clinical Social Work Practice with Children of Incarcerated Parents*, Essential Clinical Social Work Series,
https://doi.org/10.1007/978-3-031-28823-4_11

CPNYC possesses unparalleled expertise and understanding of the problems and effective interventions for use with children and families affected by incarceration. Because of the organization's singular experience working with this population, CPNYC understands, as perhaps few others can, that providing comprehensive family-strengthening services is the linchpin to recidivism prevention, positive familial relationships, and healthy outcomes for parents and children. The barriers affecting children and families of incarceration, as well as the requisite services available to them, are not widely known due to the general lack of city, state, and federal funding directed at this population. Organizations like CPNYC, which specifically serves children and families of incarceration, are not common, nor are they typically recipients of substantial government funding, which is often earmarked for more widely known justice-involved populations, such as parents who have been released from prison.

CPNYC recognizes that in order to draw this population into mental healthcare, the agency needs to create a welcoming and resourceful organization that is staffed with culturally responsive employees and practitioners. While New York City is home to several of the most remarkable community-based organizations that work with the injustice system, no other organization co-locates comprehensive youth development and family engagement service with a licensed mental health clinic at the same program site, to provide customized services that have been developed exclusively to serve the needs, interests, and concerns of families affected by parental incarceration.

Mentoring Program

Children of Promise, NYC's Peer-to-Peer Mentoring Program is at the forefront of the multi-layered and comprehensive services that our organization offers to formerly incarcerated individuals. Within its curriculum-based program, Children of Promise, NYC's trained Licensed Masters in Social Work facilitators work individually with each parent returning from prison, assigning them to a formerly incarcerated individual who is actively engaged in the community and on a well-established career and academic path. CPNYC's mentoring program is based on research and anecdotal evidence, which demonstrates that consistency and duration of a mentoring relationship are two of the most critical components in providing a context for productive relationship-building between the mentor and mentee. Their mentoring program facilitates the building of a solid mentoring relationship first, then supplements with appropriate career and academic guidance as formerly incarcerated community members assist their mentees with the transition into employment and academic settings.

The social and environmental consequences of experiencing parental incarceration for children are numerous. Because many families served at CPNYC experienced parental incarceration for much of their lives, the organization's programming uses its extensive research to address the disparities that more parents who have been incarcerated are susceptible to receiving public assistance and disruptive residential mobility, as well as developmental, social, and emotional delays that increase emotional responses to the hardships faced due to the loss of their loved ones. Because the effects of losing one's parent to incarceration increases social and emotional problems, and the experience of paternal incarceration is very different and more pronounced than other forms of the primary caretaker's absence, CPNYC's research-based mentoring program highlights the particular and acute trauma that losing one's primary caretaker to the criminal justice system creates. Seventy percent of the children in this program have lost their fathers to incarceration, and it is argued that this loss changes the family's status to that of a single-parent family, ushering in effects similar to those brought on by the death of a parent or divorce. Therefore, CPNYC has designed a mentoring program that not only pairs adults returning to the community with formerly incarcerated individuals thriving in their communities but also acknowledges the emotional harm that has been caused to the child of someone returning home.

This adult-mentoring program has been designed to restore and heal these absences that are directly a product of the criminal justice system—in particular, losing a father—as well as increasing that father's abilities to sustainably provide for his children. This program is designed for adult fathers, mothers, and caretakers to be paired with other parents in the community, to validate their experiences and walk them through the specific processes to obtain employment and education opportunities that, in turn, become a teachable opportunity to provide these supportive measures to their own children, thereby decreasing intergenerational incarceration.

CPNYC's mentoring program recognizes that intergenerational trauma experienced by the incarcerated family member often has roots in parental incarceration in their own life prior to incarceration. Many of the imprisoned parents expressed that they themselves were unable to receive mentorship or support due to their own parent's absence. Once a family successfully graduates from the program, mentors write letters of recommendation, assist with resume writing, engage in job-readiness role-play, provide exposure to different academic and employment settings, help complete online applications, set up email accounts, and provide the participants with an ongoing routine for interviews. Ultimately, this helps provide a structured schedule for formerly incarcerated individuals to participate in and offer opportunities to model this routine for their own children. Parents have shared that the skills learned from their mentor are qualities of emotional capacity and change that they then pass down to their own family members enrolled in the program. By instilling political resistance as a form of therapeutic healing, parents within the CPNYC mentoring program address how this specifically breaks the cycle of intergenerational incarceration and rates of recidivism.

CPNYC's Peer-to-Peer mentoring program delivers 5 hours a week of individual mentorship overseen by licensed mental healthcare providers. This initial year-long matching process will assist the parents in finding sustainable employment and prepare them to re-enter the workforce. After the initial year, depending on the academic and employment strides made, the mentorship focus becomes maintenance.

Three hours per week, the mentor and mentee meet to discuss the adult's progress in their field and have a safe, supportive environment to discuss any issues that may come up. Children of Promise, NYC is able to provide consistent summary reports of the participants' progress made over time to parole boards, parole officers, judges, and legal authorities as a form of advocacy and mitigation practice to challenge social myths influenced by racial bias that people return to prison due to continued detrimental choices made. Completion of this program is statistically shown to keep parents out of the criminal justice system and support their families and children. With their participation, CPNYC continues to report increased positive outcomes for all formerly incarcerated parents enrolled in their mentorship program.

Re-entry Services

Children of Promise, NYC's Family Re-entry Services provides a variety of programs to help individuals that are newly released from jail or prison to successfully navigate the challenges of re-entry, access opportunities to improve their lives (including proven protective factors, such as education and housing), and avoid recidivism. CPNYC's interventions for effective re-entry include:

- Individualized sessions to connect individuals with competitive, sustainable employment
- Connection to educational programs that promote higher learning
- Access to affordable, sustainable housing

Moreover, CPNYC maintains partnerships with a variety of local organizations, such as Vera Institute of Justice, the Prisoner Reentry Institute at John Jay College, Code Cooperative, and the Parole Preparation Project.

CPNYC has utilized mitigation practices to create a program for each parent that is reflective of the services necessary for alternative-to-incarceration opportunities. Parents are able to attend daily weekday sessions with the re-entry coordinators as well as credible messengers. These messengers are formerly incarcerated parents who have specifically designated first-hand what concrete services are essential to combat systemic oppression regularly faced by formerly incarcerated adults. Within their sessions, they address college readiness, job applications, and housing.

Parent-Centered Programming

Children of Promise, NYC's Parent Engagement Program (PEP) is an evidence-based parenting skill-training program that addresses the unique challenges facing criminal-justice-involved parents and their children. Offered in a group setting,

CPNYC's trained facilitators lead formerly incarcerated parents through narrative therapy individual and family sessions to help each parent develop a parenting plan specific to the needs of their family. The PEP program model and curriculum are adapted from Parenting Inside Out (PIO), an evidence-proven program conducted by a research team of psychologists, scientists, and policymakers from the National Institute of Mental Health and the Oregon Social Learning Center. This program has shown to significantly reduce recidivism and address racial trauma while improving family relationships and parenting skills. The core elements of the PEP curriculum are derived from Parent Management Training (PMT), an evidence-based practice cited in the Best Practice list of the American Psychological Association and the Office of Victims of Crime of the U.S. Department of Justice.

This evidence-based program series supplies formerly incarcerated caregivers with effective parenting strategies to improve caregiver-child relationships and enhance the family unit. The core components of the PEP curriculum are based on enhancing parent-child communication, problem-solving, monitoring, positive reinforcement, and healing-centered techniques. Parents involved in the program develop and refine social interactional skills and relational behaviors they can utilize in all aspects of their lives, which will help guide their children toward becoming empowered and proud adults. The PEP program gives formerly incarcerated parents a way of navigating life that uses anti-oppressive practices to highlight internal power, which strengthens their skills to interact with children, partners, co-parents, officials, friends, and family. Participants learn to celebrate the uniqueness of each person and invite others into caring and authentic relationships. With PEP training, injustice-involved adults can encourage communal healing through connection and shared realities faced by those who directly experience oppressive systems that are designed to maintain barriers to success for formerly incarcerated adults.

The Parent Engagement Program delivers a 12-month course series, Monday through Friday, each 90 minutes in duration to approximately 20 caregivers per session. The program is overseen and facilitated by psychiatrists and clinicians. The family's weekly progress reports are shared with family members, children, and anyone legally involved with the parent. This includes their own narrative of the effectiveness of the therapeutic process as well as their own drafted treatment progress, as identified by the autonomous and empowered treatment goals outlined within their individualized treatment plan. To ensure all program requirements are met by the legal obligations, each parent and family receives a certificate of completion, and their treatment progress will be submitted to the court, if requested. Once each family completes their first year of PEP, they will also be able to request participation in the second year of programming with their assigned cohort, which will continue to focus on parents healing from carceral trauma, family healing practices, individual psychotherapy, and political advocacy through the parent advisory board.

Group Psychotherapy

Trauma Responsive Support Groups are a primary modality of community building and healing at CPNYC. The evidence-informed clinical program offers services in individual, family, and group settings that are culturally responsive and integrate community evidence in their practice. The selection of evidence-informed practices acknowledges and infuses the diverse ecologies of the community served. The research-driven interventions implemented in these various clinical capacities are trauma-focused cognitive behavioral therapy, narrative therapy, and attachment-based treatment for children and adults who have been traumatically impacted by systemic racism experiences related to police violence. For the families at CPNYC, this trauma takes the form of grief and loss, which commonly produces stigma and shame associated with this complex trauma type and accompanying PTSD, anxiety, and depression.

Child-Centered Mental Health Programming

CPNYC's outpatient mental health program provides trauma-responsive, evidence-informed services for children of incarcerated parents and their families. As complex traumatic stress is prevalent in this community, CPNYC employs a variety of modalities including, but not limited to, trauma-focused cognitive behavioral therapy, behavioral therapy, narrative therapy, anti-oppressive child and group psychotherapy, mindfulness practices, and art therapy, which best support behaviors and symptoms associated with traumatic stress. This model is composed of licensed mental health counselors, Licensed Clinical Social Workers, and Licensed Master of Social Work clinicians who are trained solely to support clients in individual psychotherapy sessions, family therapy sessions, and group therapy sessions. The program is overseen by psychiatrists and senior clinicians who employ critical consciousness and culture-based countertransference supervision to ensure that each clinician is culturally responsive to the urgent experiences of each child within the program.

Caregivers, incarcerated parents, and their children collectively achieve better long-term outcomes when they are autonomously encouraging their own family narrative and framework to design a path to develop healthy family relationships and to address the issues and challenges of incarceration in a family context. Research shows that the presence of an incarcerated parent is crucial to cultivating the individual's sense of safety and support and to soothing anxiety and depression as a way to address psychological and emotional needs. The CPNYC anti-racist therapeutic modeling for children reinforces that a major component of the psychological healing of children and adolescents with incarcerated parents is the presence of the parent, as well as the repair of their relationship. CPNYC's family therapy design nurtures change and development, as it focuses on family relationships as a critical factor in an individual's mental health, which is exactly why the program includes family therapy sessions. The involvement of parents in the challenges of the individual benefits the feelings of success and power shared by each child. This therapeutic program model and design encompasses best practices narratively framed by children and their families as the most culturally responsive, with advocacy practice as the leading example throughout the United States to combat mass incarceration and offer a space to children who are otherwise dismissed and devalued by the greater society.

Conclusion

The growing number of children suffering the loss of parental incarceration in countries like the United States is unprecedented (Murray et al., 2012). There is an urgency within both clinical and therapeutic settings to prioritize identifying and understanding the possible effects on children as clinicians work to expand practice knowledge on primary trauma associated with grief and loss. It is evident that children with incarcerated parents are at heightened risk for systemic oppressive harm and disenfranchisement as intergenerational cycles of mass incarceration plague Black and Brown communities.

In therapeutic practice, relatively little is still known or considered about the causal effects of parental incarceration on children (Murray et al., 2012). Therefore, this unpacking and deeper understanding of great loss warrants large-scale investment to understand why children develop extreme social, emotional, and psychological strain and challenges after parental incarceration, and clinicians must identify how harmful effects can be prevented.

An Integrated Approach to Clinical Social Work Practice with Children of Incarcerated Parents is a call to action for practitioners to embody clinical change in their therapeutic approach and style which will now recognize and amplify the silenced emotional, psychological, familial, communal, and societal impacts of mass incarceration. This therapeutic advancement in clinical practice will engage children and families in ways that prioritize and center their voice, unique experiences, and re-define the social work and mental health values of individuals truly being the experts in not only their own lives, but in their own healing. Children of incarcerated parents seek recognition and honoring of their trauma, which will inevitably expand clinical care and a demand that new practices include their powerful narrative of hope. This child-centered healing will break the cycle of systemic violence causing their pain to go unnoticed or remain silenced. There is an opportunity to mobilize therapeutic practice and prioritize the voices of children most impacted, which will lead to therapeutic repair and necessary changes within the mental health system at large.

This book is a call to action for practitioners to embody clinical change in their therapeutic approach to recognize and amplify the silenced emotional, psychological, familial, communal, and societal impacts of mass incarceration. This advancement in clinical practice will engage children and families in ways that center their voice and experiences and redefine the mental health values of individuals truly being the experts not only in their own lives, but also in their own healing.

Reflection Questions

1. Putting all of your learning together: Create your own community-based model for children of incarcerated parents. In this model, you create what activities, therapies, modalities, and policies would be at the center of this organization.
2. If you could replicate this model in other states, what information would be pertinent to train the clinicians and administrators working with children of incarcerated parents?
3. How would your program or design disrupt mass incarceration while healing the individual child and family?
4. How has policy shaped your clinical practice?
5. As a call to action: Where will you start today in changing your clinical style and which therapeutic practice and core concept listed throughout this guide will you incorporate into your social work practice?

References

Children of Promise, NYC. http://www.cpncyc.org/

Murray, J., Farrington, D. P., & Sekol, I. (2012). Children's antisocial behavior, mental health, drug use, and educational performance after parental incarceration: A systematic review and meta-analysis. *Psychological Bulletin, 138*(2): 175–210.

Chapter 12
Conclusion

The growing number of children suffering the loss of parental incarceration in countries like the United States is unprecedented (Murray et al., 2012). There is an urgency within both clinical and therapeutic settings to prioritize identifying and understanding the possible effects on children as clinicians work to expand practice knowledge on primary trauma associated with grief and loss. It is evident that children with incarcerated parents are at heightened risk for systemic oppressive harm and disenfranchisement as intergenerational cycles of mass incarceration plague Black and Brown communities. In therapeutic practice, relatively little is still known or considered about the causal effects of parental incarceration on children (Murray et al., 2012). Therefore, this unpacking and deeper understanding of great loss warrants large-scale investment to understand why children develop extreme social, emotional, and psychological strain and challenges after parental incarceration, and clinicians must identify how harmful effects can be prevented.

An Integrated Approach to Clinical Social Work Practice with Children of Incarcerated Parents is a call to action for practitioners to embody clinical change in their therapeutic approach and style which will now recognize and amplify the silenced emotional, psychological, familial, communal, and societal impacts of mass incarceration. This therapeutic advancement in clinical practice will engage children and families in ways that prioritize and center their voice, unique experiences, and re-define the social work and mental health values of individuals truly being the experts in not only their own lives, but in their own healing. Children of incarcerated parents seek recognition and honoring of their trauma which will inevitably expand clinical care and demand that new practices include their powerful narrative of hope. This child-centered healing will break the cycle of systemic violence causing their pain to go unnoticed or remain silenced. There is an opportunity to mobilize therapeutic practice and prioritize the voices of children most impacted, which will lead to therapeutic repair and necessary changes within the mental health system at large.

A. Morgan-Mullane, *An Integrative Approach to Clinical Social Work Practice with Children of Incarcerated Parents*, Essential Clinical Social Work Series,
https://doi.org/10.1007/978-3-031-28823-4_12

Reference

Murray, J., Farrington, D. P., & Sekol, I. (2012). Children's antisocial behavior, mental health, drug use, and educational performance after parental incarceration: A systematic review and meta-analysis. *Psychological Bulletin, 138*(2), 175–210

Index

A. Morgan-Mullane, *An Integrative Approach to Clinical Social Work Practice with Children of Incarcerated Parents*, Essential Clinical Social Work Series,
https://doi.org/10.1007/978-3-031-28823-4_8

CPSIA information can be obtained
at www.ICGtesting.com
Printed in the USA
LVHW080454050623
748857LV00006B/305

9 783031 288227